WILTSHIRE

TEASHOP WALKS

Jean Patefield

COUNTRYSIDE BOOKS
NEWBURY BERKSHIRE

First published 2009
© Jean Patefield 2009

COUNTRYSIDE BOOKS
3 Catherine Road
Newbury, Berkshire

To view our complete range of books,
please visit us at
www.countrysidebooks.co.uk

ISBN 978 1 84674 144 9

Produced through MRM Associates Ltd., Reading
Typeset by Mac Style, Beverley, E. Yorkshire
Printed in Thailand

*All material for the manufacture of this book
was sourced from sustainable forests.*

Contents

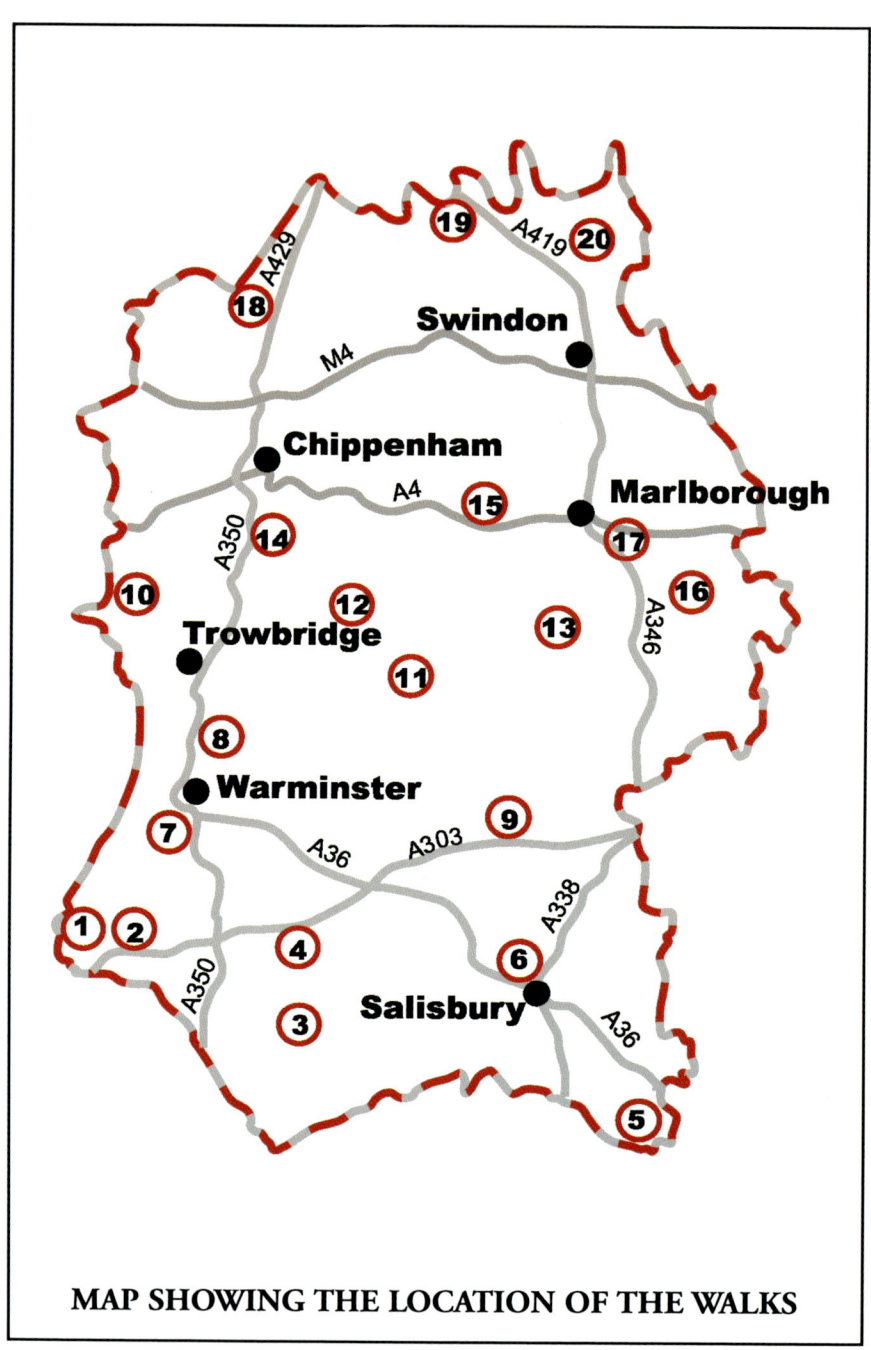

MAP SHOWING THE LOCATION OF THE WALKS

INTRODUCTION

Wiltshire is an outstanding county for walking, with rolling hills that fold gently into the landscape, panoramic plains fringed with dramatic downland and broad fertile valleys that are home to some of England's prettiest and most charming villages. The twenty walks in this book explore all of these landscapes from the southern edge of the Cotswolds (Walks 18 and 19) to the northern fringe of the New Forest (Walk 5).

It is impossible to visit Wiltshire and not be aware of the long history of England. The awe-inspiring and mysterious remains of ancient civilisations never fail to intrigue (Walks 8, 9 and 15) and some walks use the routes our pre-historic ancestors followed (Walks 2 and 15). Evidence of more recent history from the Romans (Walks 6 and 17) through the bloody turmoil of the Saxons and Danes (Walks 8 and 13) is widespread. Medieval strongholds (Walks 2, 3, 6, 12 and 18) tell of rival barons, bloody skirmishes and courtly intrigue. Towering cathedrals (Walk 6) and mighty abbeys (Walk 14 and 18) reveal the pre-Reformation Church's immense power. In more recent centuries great wealth has led to magnificent estates and gardens (Walks 1, 4, and 7) and these are now available for everyone to enjoy. While the Industrial Revolution bypassed much of Wiltshire, there are many fascinating reminders of our industrial heritage (Walks 10, 12 and, especially, 16).

Wiltshire offers a great variety of walks to suit every occasion and mood. Most people enjoy waterside walks and in Wiltshire these include rivers (Walks 6, 14 and 18), canals, notably the attractive Kennet and Avon (Walks 10, 12, 13 and 16) and lakes (Walks 1, 4, 7 and particularly 19). Some walks climb the Downs and there are many with breathtaking views (notably Walks 1, 2, 8, 11, and 12). Wiltshire is home to one of England's most ancient forests (Walk 17) and there is plenty of good woodland walking to enjoy (Walks 1, 7 and 16).

There are some charming villages just waiting to be explored, many complete with thatched roofs and roses round the door (Walks 11, 14, 16 and 20). Many of Wiltshire's towns are brimming with character and individuality and have pleasant walking routes into the heart of them (Walk 6, 10, 12, 17 and 18).

Tea is often said to be the best meal to eat out in England and I believe tea is a meal to be enjoyed on all possible occasions. The custom of afternoon tea is said to have been invented by Anna, Duchess of Bedford, in about 1840. She often became peckish in the late afternoon – don't we all? –and invited her friends to join her in a snack of sandwiches and cake.

Scones with clotted cream and strawberry jam, delicious home-made cakes, toasted teacakes dripping with butter in winter, delicate cucumber sandwiches in summer all washed down with the cup that cheers are some of the best, typically English food available and often excellent value. Bad for the figure maybe, but the walking will see to that.

Tea is not only refreshing during a walk; it is good for you! In Scotland apothecaries sold it and it was available on prescription on form number 99. This is the origin of the name of one famous brand. Another, Typhoo, is the Chinese word for doctor.

The best teashops serve a range of cakes, all home-made and including fruit cake, as well as scones and other temptations. Teapots should be capacious and pour properly. Many of the teashops visited on these walks fulfil all these criteria admirably and they all offer a good cup of tea. With one exception (Walk 3), they all have at least light lunches available as well so there is no need to think of these walks as just something for the afternoons.

There are many excellent establishments in Wiltshire but even so, teashops are not scattered evenly throughout the county. In some popular places, the visitor is spoilt for choice. In such cases the most convenient teashop that, in the author's opinion, most closely fulfils the criteria set out above is recommended but should that not appeal, there are others from which to choose. In other places where there is a delightful walk to be enjoyed, the choice for tea is more limited. However, they all offer a good tea part way round an attractive walk. The opening times and telephone number of each teashop are given.

The pleasures of summer walking are obvious. Many of the teashops featured in this book have an attractive garden where tea can be taken outside when the weather is suitable. However, let me urge you not to overlook the pleasures of a good walk in winter. The roads and paths are quieter and what could be better than sitting by an open fire in a cosy teashop scoffing crumpets that you can enjoy with a clear conscience due to the brisk walk to get them! Be aware that many teashops are rather vague about when they open out of season: it seems to depend on weather and mood. If you are planning a walk on a wet November Tuesday, for example, a call to check that tea will actually be available that day is a wise precaution. Some are definitely closed outside the summer season or during the week and for these walks, where possible, an alternative source of refreshment is given. In most cases, these are pubs serving food, which in some cases includes tea.

The twenty walks in this book are all between 3½ and 7 miles long and should be well within the capacity of the average person, including those of mature years and families with children. They are intended to take the walker through this attractive corner of England at a gentle pace with plenty of time to stop and stare, to savour the beauty and interest all around. A dedicated yomper and stomper could probably knock off the whole book in a single weekend but in doing so they would have missed the point and seen nothing. To fully appreciate the countryside it is necessary to go slowly with your eyes and ears open.

Some of the walks are short and level, ideal for a pipe opener on a winter's day, or giving plenty of time to dawdle away a summer's afternoon. Others are longer or more strenuous, some making an excellent all day expedition. Certain of the walks involve a little climbing. This is inevitable as the hills add enormous interest and with no ascents, there are no views. However, this presents no problem to the sensible walker who has three uphill gears – slowly, very slowly and admiring the view.

All the routes are on public rights of way or permissive paths and have been carefully checked but, of course, in the countryside things do change; a stile replaces a gate, for example, or a wood is extended. A sketch map illustrates each walk and they are all circular. An Ordnance Survey map is useful as well, especially for identifying the main features of views. The Explorer 1:25,000 (2½ inches to 1 mile) series are by far the best maps to use for walking. Sheets 118, 130, 131, 142, 143, 156, 157, 168, 169 and a tiny bit of OL 22 cover the walks in this book. The grid reference of the starting point and the appropriate maps are given for each walk.

Of course, it behoves us all to remember that the place where we take our recreation is other people's workplace and act with consideration to those who depend on the countryside for their livelihood and make their homes there.

The walks, all starting somewhere a car can be parked, are designed so that the teashop is reached in the second half so a really good appetite for tea can be worked up and then its effects walked off. However, it sometimes fits in better with the plans for the day to start and finish at the teashop and so for each walk there are details of how to do this.

So put on your walking shoes and prepare to be delighted by the charms of Wiltshire and refreshed by a traditional English tea!

Jean Patefield

Walk 1

STOURHEAD

*T*he gardens at Stourhead are widely recognised as a triumph of landscape architecture and thousands flock there every year to enjoy the artfully created vistas. Beyond the gardens lies the heavily wooded estate and this is equally beautiful, albeit in a less regulated way. This walk explores the estate and includes some outstanding woodland walking coupled with superb views and I cannot recommend it too highly. Most of the way is on well-made tracks and paths so the going underfoot is easy, enabling one to more fully enjoy the surroundings. The return is along a carefully graded carriageway constructed in the 18th century for the pleasure of those staying at the house and equally enjoyable on foot in the 21st century – perhaps even more so now the beeches that line the route have reached their full maturity.

The National Trust can be relied upon for excellent refreshments and this is no exception. The restaurant at Stourhead is housed in a large, airy building and there are plenty of seats outside. They offer a tempting range of cakes and, of course, cream teas are served. For lunch

9

there is a good choice of sandwiches and salads and full lunches are served from 11.30 am. They are open every day except Christmas Day, between 10 am and 5.30 pm in the summer, opening a little later and closing earlier in the winter. Telephone: 01747 841152.

Teas are also served in the garden of Stourton House adjacent to the National Trust car park and open on Wednesday, Thursday and Sunday in the summer.

DISTANCE: 6 miles

MAP: OS Explorer 142 Shepton Mallet & Mendip Hills East

STARTING POINT: National Trust car park for King Alfred's Tower (GR 748353).

HOW TO GET THERE: From the B3092, Frome to Mere road, about ¹/₃ mile north of the turning for Stourton, follow the signs for King Alfred's Tower to a car park on the right, which is not well signed at the time of writing.

ALTERNATIVE STARTING POINT: If you wish to visit the teashop at the beginning or end of your walk, start in Stourton where there is ample parking in the National Trust car park. The teashop is adjacent to the car park. You will then start the walk at point 5.

THE WALK

1 Return to the road and take a track opposite. Walk along this lovely woodland track for about ¹/₂ mile. When the main track bends left, continue in the same direction on a downhill track. Join a track coming in from the left and continue ahead for 50 yards to a cross track.

King Alfred's Tower was built as a landscape feature to commemorate the end of the Seven Years War against France and the accession of King George III. It supposedly stands near the location of Egbert's Stone, where it is said that King Alfred rallied the Saxons in May AD 878 before the important Battle of Ethandun (see Walk 8). On 10th July 1944 a military plane heading for Zeals airfield and carrying five American airmen flew into the conical roof of the turret in thick fog and all were killed. The turret was repaired in 1986. The tower is 160 ft high and there are 205 steps to the top: the views are magnificent on a clear day. It is open to the public every day between 11.30 am and 4.30 pm from mid March to the end of October (charge).

2 Turn left, shortly passing a barn on the right, and follow the track to a T-junction.

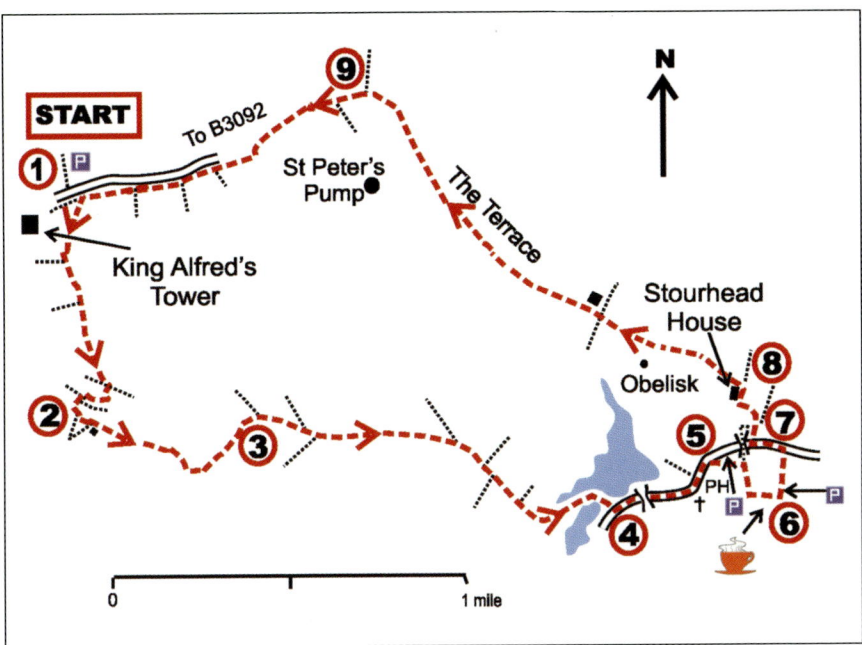

The National Trust do not own this part of the Stourhead estate and it remains in the hands of the Hoare family. It is a Tax-Exempt Heritage Asset, which means that the owner has given an undertaking to the Inland Revenue to preserve the character of the land and allow reasonable public access in exchange for exemption from inheritance tax. The woodlands are managed both for timber and conservation.

3 Turn right. Ignore a track on the left and then one on the right and go ahead to shortly find a stile by a gate out of the woodland. Keep ahead by a fence on the right to another gate and through this go ahead, once more on a track. Press on, signed 'Turner's Paddock', as a track joins from the left. Carry on along this track, eventually passing a small lake with a waterfall, to a T-junction with a lane.

This lake was artificially created by the dam in 1754. The waterfall was added in 1766 as a decorative way of carrying surplus water down from the main lake.

4 Turn left, signed 'Stourton', passing under a rock arch.

The world-famous garden of Stourhead may be glimpsed from the lane and is an outstanding triumph of English landscape art. The cavalcade of breathtaking vistas has matured to surprise, inspire and entrance in a way that would make its creator, Henry Hoare II, a proud man. His garden has been nurtured by his successors and has matured into the living work of art he sought to create nearly three centuries ago. Now cared for by the National Trust, the garden is open to the public throughout the year and is well worth visiting. Telephone: 01747 841152.

5 Turn right into the courtyard of the Spread Eagle pub. Go through an arch, across a small car park and follow the zig-zag path up to the restaurant.

6 From the restaurant, go left through the car park to a lane and turn left to the gateway to Stourhead House.

7 Turn right through a wooden 'turnstile' next to the gate and walk beside the driveway and in front of the house to gates and a cattle grid.

Henry Hoare I bought Stourhead from the Stourton family in 1717. The family fortune had been founded by Richard Hoare. He started as a goldsmith in London in 1672 and founded a bank in 1690. This has survived the turbulent centuries since and is England's oldest privately-owned bank, still owned by the Hoare family. The original manor house was demolished and a new one built between 1720 and 1724. Over the next 200 years the Hoare family collected many heirlooms, including a large library and art collection. In 1901 the house was gutted by fire. However, many of the treasures were saved, and the house was rebuilt in a near identical style. The last Hoare family member to own the property, Henry Hugh Arthur Hoare, gave Stourhead House and gardens to the National Trust in 1946. It is open to the public between mid March and early November from 11.30 am to 4.30 pm every day except Wednesday and Thursday.

8 Through the gates, turn left along a track signed 'Alfred's Tower' and follow this to a lodge, passing the Obelisk to the left. Continue past the lodge and through a gate to keep ahead on a wide, grassy path, the Terrace.

9 After about a mile, follow the path as it bears round to the left and pass the top of Six Wells Valley on the left. Press on until King Alfred's Tower comes into view and, at an information board, turn right back to the road and the car park. (If you started at Stourhead, turn left along the track.)

Walk 2

WHITE SHEET HILL AND MERE

*H*undreds *of years before Roman engineers drove their famous straight roads across the landscape, the ancient Britons followed a network of trade routes, often keeping to hilltops. This walk at the western edge of the high plateau of Salisbury Plain joins one of these as it passes a Neolithic earthwork and Iron Age fort. There are extensive views across the Wiltshire countryside and south towards Dorset so a clear day for this walk is a must. The route drops down to the pleasant old coaching town of Mere for refreshment, visiting the site of a medieval castle on the way, so this is a very interesting expedition.*

Angel Corner is an attractive modern teashop in an 18th-century building in the heart of Mere and meets the needs of this busy community. The cakes are displayed in a cabinet and you are sure to be tempted by an old favourite such as coffee and walnut cake or something more unusual such as, on my visit, orange and sultana cake. For lunch there is a choice of sandwiches and filled jacket potatoes, as well as salads and things on toast. These are supplemented by daily specials, including special sandwich fillings. Angel Corner also stocks an unusual range of African crafts, all sourced directly from the makers, reflecting the owner's interest in Africa. The teashop is open throughout the year, just closing on Tuesdays in winter and Sunday and Bank Holidays all year. Telephone: 01747 860187.

When the teashop is closed there are several pubs in Mere that serve food.

DISTANCE: 5^1/$_2$ miles

MAPS: OS Explorer 142 Shepton Mallet & Mendip Hills East and 143 Warminster & Trowbridge

STARTING POINT: White Sheet Hill parking area (GR 797349)

HOW TO GET THERE: From the B3092, Mere to Maiden Bradley road, at the Red Lion Inn 2^1/$_2$ miles north of its junction with the A303, take a tiny, unsigned lane east to an unsigned parking area on the right at the point where the lane becomes a roughly surfaced track.

ALTERNATIVE STARTING POINT: If you wish to visit the teashop at the beginning or end of your walk, start in Mere where there are two signed car parks. The teashop is in The Square near the George Hotel. You will then start the walk at point 5.

THE WALK

1 With your back to the lane, take a path on the right that leads down to a gate, then up to and through a small wood on a knoll. Continue downhill to a gate and stile across the path.

There is a war memorial at the top of the hill on the left of the path. During the Second World War there was an RAF base near Zeals, a few miles west of here. The RAF Glider Pick-up Unit used it for training in February 1945. The aim was to recover gliders that had landed in inaccessible places during the invasion of Europe. A Dakota tug aircraft flew very low to pick up a towrope suspended just above the ground on poles, to snatch the glider into the air without the tug landing. At the completion of the first training course on 19th February 1945, the air and ground crew took off to return to their home base at RAF Leicester East. Beech Knoll was covered in cloud that day and the aircraft flew into it, killing all on board, except the pilot who died later of severe injuries. This memorial was dedicated in 1999 in the presence of 150 relatives and guests, including representatives of the British, Australian and Canadian Air Forces.

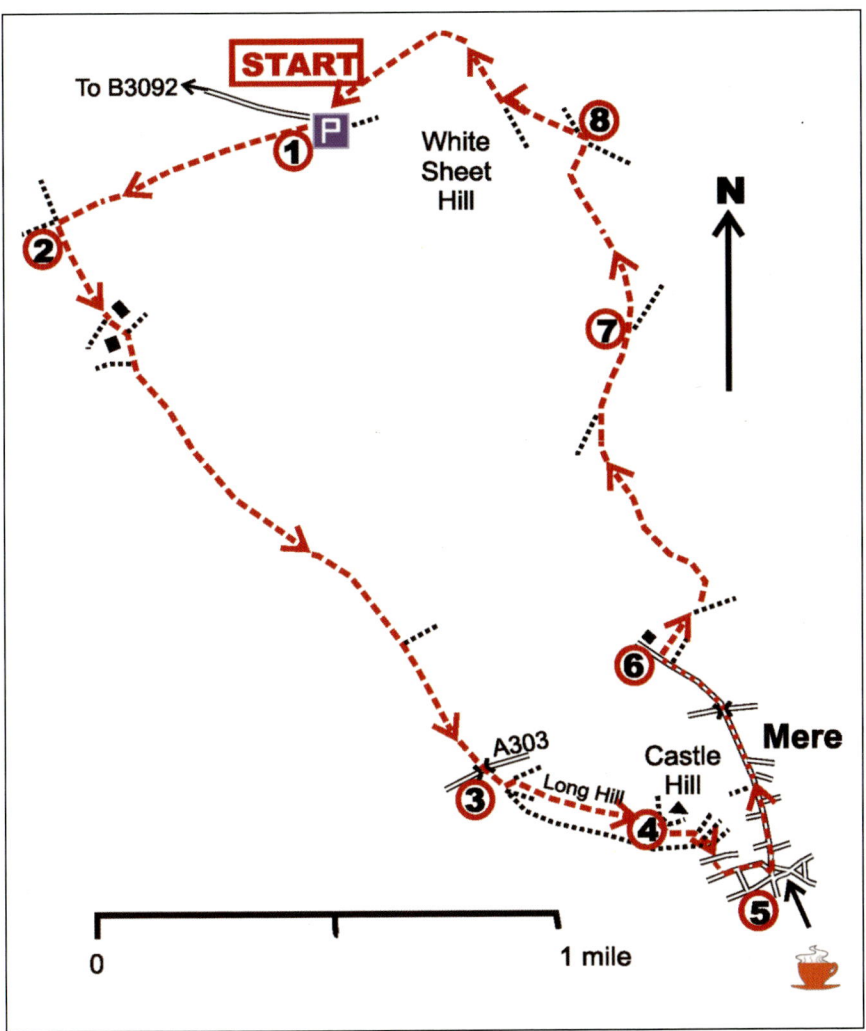

2 Through the gate, turn left through a field gate on the left to walk along the left-hand side of a field and then past a farm. Cross the farm drive and continue ahead on a track, passing a cottage on the left. Press on along the track, through a gateway, and go forward, initially with a hedge on the right, to eventually reach a bridge over the A303.

3 Cross the bridge. After 20 yards take the left option at a fork and after a further 40 yards go through a metal kissing gate next to a field gate.

15

The wonderful Wiltshire countryside along the way.

Climb up Long Hill and follow the path along the top of the hill to a kissing gate.

In 1252 Henry III granted his brother Richard, Earl of Cornwall, permission to build a castle on the hill above his manor of Mere. The building was of Chilmark stone and 200 oak trees were used in the construction. It was 309 ft long by 102 ft wide, with six towers. It was by no means the Earl's main residence; he was one of the wealthiest men in Europe at the time, as well as being King of Germany, and had estates all over the place. He apparently used it as a stud farm for his warhorses. By the 17th century the castle was a ruin and its stone was used in many buildings in Mere. There is nothing left to see of this mighty structure but it is worth making the climb to the top of Castle Hill for the view.

④ Through the gate, bear right down some steps, then follow the path along the castle mound. When the path bears left, go down a second set of steps, across a lower path and down a third set. At the bottom, bear right beside a recreation ground then along a passageway between buildings to a road. Turn left into the centre of Mere and the teashop in The Square.

Today Mere is a very pleasant small town because, though it lies on a major route to the south-west, it is spared the burden of heavy traffic as the A303 has been re-routed round the town. However, it owes much of its prosperity and appearance to its position on the coach route from London to Exeter. In 1750 the journey from Mere to London took 24 hours and cost 30 shillings inside and 16 shillings exposed to the weather outside the coach. As well as being a centre for the surrounding country, a role it still fulfils today, Mere was also a noted centre for linen and silk production until the end of the 19th century.

⑤ From the teashop cross The Square and take the small road opposite. Follow this out of Mere and over the A303.

⑥ Immediately before some cottages on the right, turn right on a signed bridleway along a surfaced track. When the surfaced track bends right, keep more or less ahead on a rough track and follow this as it wends its way up the hill, with ever-widening views opening up.

⑦ Almost at the top of the hill, go through a field gate on the left and walk along the top of the steep slope to a fenced mound, topped by a communication mast on the left. At this point turn right across the field to a gate onto a track.

The ditch around White Sheet Hill on the left encloses 15 acres of what was an Iron Age hill fort. To the south and west the steep slope protected the site so there was only a single ditch. The north and east sides faced the level plateau and had a triple ditch. The name comes from the Old English word scoot, *meaning steep place. When the hill fort was in use the slope was kept clear of vegetation and would have been bright white due to the chalk – a landmark for miles around.*

⑧ Turn left along the track back to the start.

This track is part of the ancient trade route known as the Harrow Way that crossed southern England from Kent to Devon and dates back into the mists of time, probably to the Stone Age. It is not an accident that it passes the Iron Age hill fort and a much earlier Stone Age earthwork. An information board by the track explains the latter. It later became a road for transporting lead mined in the Mendips and, later still, for driving sheep and cattle from the west to market at Wilton and Salisbury. It was a turnpike road for which travellers had to pay a toll and has milestones along the route dated 1750: there is one on the right just before the car park.

Walk 3

OLD AND NEW WARDOUR CASTLES

This walk explores one of the prettiest corners of Wiltshire. It starts at a romantic ruin of a castle, artistically preserved as such to be a feature in the landscape of its successor. The walk between the two is charming. This is followed by some delightful stretches of woodland walking connected by tiny lanes, before refreshment at a teashop with a great view of the downs. This delightful walk lies within the West Wiltshire and Cranbourne Chase Area of Outstanding Natural Beauty and I am sure you will agree that the designation is justified.

Ansty Farm Shop Tea Room is exactly what its name suggests. The shop stocks a range of excellent cakes and pastries and you may choose one to enjoy with your pot of tea. Cream teas are also served. It is literally a tearoom, with no sandwiches or other options for lunch so you need to time this walk to arrive at teatime! There are some tables outside overlooking the Pick Your Own area with a great view of the downs beyond. They are open every day except Monday between 9.30 am and 5.30 pm (4 pm on Sundays) throughout the year and Mondays as well in June and July. Telephone: 01747 829072.

There is no other source of refreshment on this walk.

DISTANCE: $4^1/_2$ miles

MAP: OS Explorer 118 Shaftesbury & Cranbourne Chase

STARTING POINT: Old Wardour Castle car park (GR 938264)

HOW TO GET THERE: The castle is about 2 miles south of Tisbury, as the crow flies, in a maze of little lanes. From Tisbury take the road signed 'Wardour Ansty Swallowfield' past the station and follow the brown tourist signs to Old Wardour Castle.

ALTERNATIVE STARTING POINT: If you wish to visit the teashop at the beginning or end of your walk, start at Ansty Farm Shop on the A30 where permission must be sought before leaving your car for a lengthy period. You will then start the walk at point 6, turning right along the road.

THE WALK

1 Take a surfaced drive to the right of the castle and continue on as this becomes a track along the edge of a wood.

Old Wardour Castle.

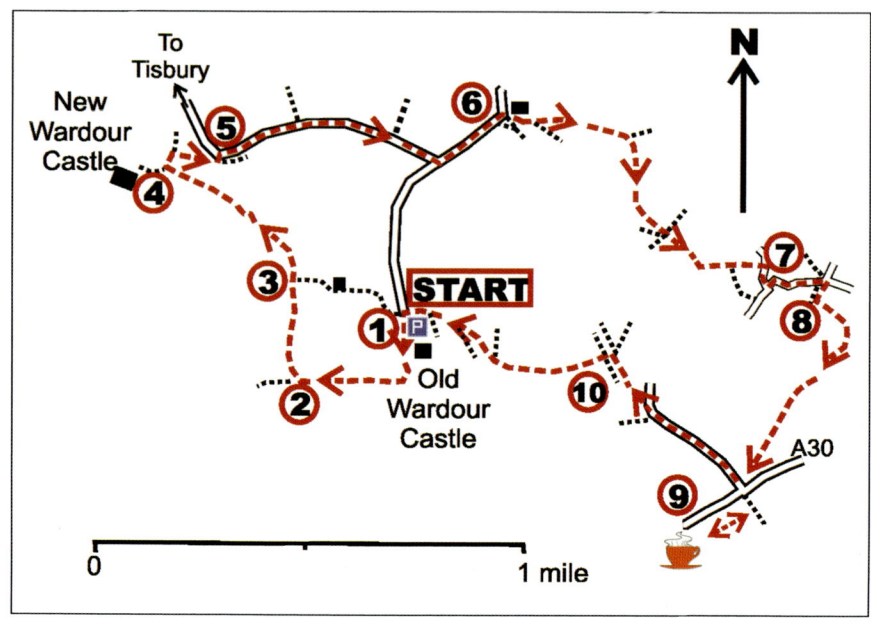

Old Wardour Castle is in the care of English Heritage and is well worth exploring. It is open to the public every day in the summer and at weekends between November and March. Telephone: 01747 870487. The history of the castle begins when John, Lord Lovell, became the owner of the manor at the end of the 14th century. Prior to this, the estate had belonged to the nunnery at Wilton Abbey. Lord Lovell was married to an heiress whose cousins were the half-brothers of King Richard II and the Lovells were amongst the wealthiest families in England. They owned extensive estates and houses all over England but Old Wardour was intended to surpass these. It was built at a time when the emphasis was shifting from defence to style and comfort. The unusual hexagonal structure was probably influenced by contemporary French design. The Lovells supported the losing Lancastrian cause in the Wars of the Roses and as a result had their estates confiscated when Edward of York became king in 1461. After a succession of owners, the wealthy and influential Arundell family bought the castle in 1547. The castle was confiscated when Sir Thomas was executed for treason in 1552, but was later acquired by his son, Sir Matthew Arundell, in 1570. By this time the house had gone from a very modern, even daring, design to being old-fashioned and uncomfortable by the standards of the day and Sir Matthew set about an Elizabethan makeover. Doorways were redesigned and windows enlarged to let in more light; a new

gallery was added and the house was decorated and furnished to a very high standard. It was badly damaged in the Civil War and was never lived in again.

2 Just before the track bends left at a magnificent oak tree on the right, turn right along a fenced track.

3 When the track bends right towards farm buildings, go over a stile on the left next to a field gate. Walk along the right-hand side of a field. Continue in the same direction when the fence on the right ends, to another stile by a gate. Over the stile, go ahead to a T-junction with a track after 25 yards.

New Wardour Castle was built in the 18th century for the Arundell family in the Palladian-style by architect James Paine, with additional pieces from Giacomo Quarenghi, who was a principal architect of St Petersburg. The famous landscape architect, Lancelot 'Capability' Brown, was hired to transform the grounds and he preserved the old castle as a landscape feature and built a banqueting house in the shadow of the ruins. After the last Lord Arundell died in 1944 the building became home to a girls' school. The school closed in 1990 when the building was sold and converted into luxury apartments so it is not open to the public.

4 Turn right, away from New Wardour Castle, for 50 yards. Immediately before a laurel hedge on both sides, turn right on a path through a wood for about 200 yards, then turn left to emerge on a lane.

5 Turn right along the lane. Ignore a turning to the right on a left-hand bend (leading to Old Wardour Castle) and carry on along the lane to where it starts to go downhill, as far as a cottage on the right by two tracks, signed 'Restricted Byway'.

6 Turn right along the left-hand track. When the way forks after 100 yards, take the left option to keep on in the same direction on a path that leads downhill through a wood. Take the right option at the next fork and keep ahead at a 5-way junction to eventually reach a stile out of the wood. Press on in the same direction across two fields to a stile onto a lane.

7 Turn right. At a T-junction turn left as far as two tracks on the right, opposite a tiny lane on the left.

21

8 Take the left-hand track. Follow it up through woodland, then round a right-hand bend, ignoring field gates to left and right, to eventually emerge in a field. Continue along the left-hand side of the field, then bear left diagonally across the corner of the next field to a stile. Maintain the same direction over a third field to a stile onto a tiny lane. Turn left to a main road, then right along the road verge for 250 yards to Ansty Farm Shop and Tea Room on the left.

9 From the teashop, retrace your steps to the lane and turn left along it. When the lane bears right downhill, continue ahead along a track to an obvious cross path.

10 Turn left. Follow the path between fields, then down through woodland to the car park where this walk started.

The most dramatic period in the history of the castle came during the Civil War. In late April 1643, Sir Edward Hungerford and a Parliamentary force of some 1,300 men besieged the castle. With her husband supporting King Charles I at Oxford and despite having only 25 troops and some household staff, 61-year-old Lady Blanche Arundell refused to surrender. The attackers' cannons inflicted only minor damage and Hungerford ordered his men to plant gunpowder mines underneath the castle walls. They laid one in the service tunnel that led to the cellars under the eastern side of the main entrance and another in the base of a latrine chute that drained the private apartments. The building resisted the explosions, but the garrison persuaded Lady Blanche to surrender on 2nd May. The Parliamentary troops promptly moved into the castle. Lord Arundell had died of wounds, and his son, Henry, 3rd Lord Arundell, laid siege to retake the castle in December 1643. Unlike the siege earlier in the year, this lasted for several months. Pounding by cannons broke windows and gouged the walls, but the castle remained strong until mid-March. Apparently, one of the occupying forces unwittingly tossed a match into a tunnel that had been mined. The resulting explosion ripped a gaping wound in the rear of the building, and destroyed the upper floors of the castle. After four days, the threat of more mining and their increasing hunger forced the Parliamentarians to admit defeat. Henry, Lord Arundell, had indeed regained control of his castle, but at the expense of its destruction. Lady Blanche retired to a life of seclusion at Winchester but is said to still haunt the castle.

Walk 4

FONTHILL BISHOP

The landscape round Fonthill Bishop is truly delightful, with abundant woodland set in rolling hills. The woodland is interspersed with fields so there are many attractive views, some of which are enhanced by the lake where you start your walk. In fact, though it is a close decision, I think this is the most charming walk in the book.

Calling in at a superb teashop three-quarters of the way round the route only adds to the enjoyment of this outstanding walk. The River Barn in Fonthill Bishop styles itself as a café and bistro, and offers a very enterprising and tempting menu. The cakes are delicious and cream teas with clotted cream are served, but I think it is worth trying to time this walk to enjoy lunch at the River Barn. As well as great sandwiches such as Somerset brie with grapes, they serve interesting light bites such as fig, prosciutto and grape salad or smoked trout parcels with salad and crusty bread, as well as seasonal daily specials. The puddings on offer are as tempting as the cakes. The traditional interior is charming and also houses the village post office and there is a spacious garden with part of it overlooking the river. It is open between 10 am and 5 pm every day except Wednesday throughout the year. Telephone: 01747 820232.

DISTANCE: 4 miles
MAP: OS Explorer 143 Warminster & Trowbridge
STARTING POINT: Lay-by near Fonthill Lake (GR 933317)
HOW TO GET THERE: Fonthill Bishop is signed from the A303 and is on the B3089, Wilton–Hindon road. From Fonthill Bishop take a minor road south, signed 'Fonthill Gifford Tisbury', for 3/4 mile to a lay-by on the left.
ALTERNATIVE STARTING POINT: If you wish to visit the teashop at the beginning or end of your walk, start in Fonthill Bishop. The River Barn has a car park but permission should be sought before leaving a car and there are other spots where a car can be parked without causing inconvenience. The teashop is on the main road in the centre of the village. You will then start the walk at point 9.

THE WALK

1 Go through a gap in the fence and follow a path beside the lake. Stay on the path as it turns left to reach a track.

Fonthill Lake is about a mile long and was created by damming a tributary of the river Nadder.

2 Turn left along the track to continue round the end of the lake.

3 Some 50 yards after the outlet from the lake, turn right on a signed path away from the lake. Walk along this for about 60 yards. Turn left on a signed path, going uphill through trees and almost back on yourself. (Not the unsigned path going uphill but in the same direction 10 yards further along the track.) On emerging in a field, turn right up beside the wood and continue along the right-hand side of the field when the wood ends.

4 At the end of the field turn left, still with a wood on the right. Ignore the first path on the right and carry on along the top of the field, with excellent views to the left, to a second, signed path at the end of the wood. Turn right along this path, still beside the wood, to a T-junction with a cross track.

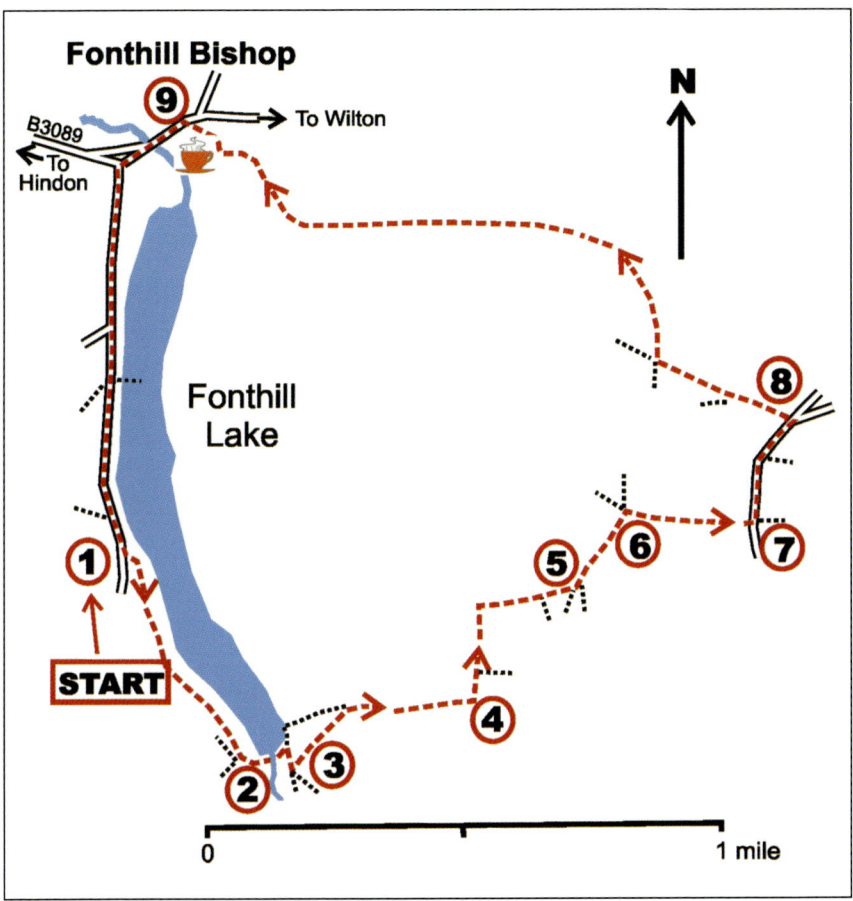

5 Turn left to a T-junction with a surfaced drive.

6 Turn right to a lane.

7 Turn left along the lane, down into a dip and up the other side to a track on the left just before a junction.

8 Turn left on a signed bridleway along the track. After some 200 yards, bear right at a fork to stay on the signed bridleway. After about ¼ mile follow the main track round to the right. Stay on this track as it climbs out of the wood, then shortly continue beside another wood to

25

eventually descend to the main road in Fonthill Bishop. Turn left to the teashop almost immediately on the left.

9 Turn left out of the teashop, along the road. Take the first road on the left, shortly passing beneath an ornate arch, and follow this back to the start.

In the 18th century the Fonthill estate was owned by the fabulously wealthy Beckford family and was inherited by William Beckford at the age of ten in 1770. Few men gained greater notoriety in the late 18th and early 19th centuries than the 'Fool of Fonthill'. His homosexual activities scandalised polite society and he was forced to flee abroad where he travelled in such style that he was often mistaken for the Emperor of Austria. He had already married and his young wife joined him in exile and died in childbirth. On his return to England he set about creating a gothic fantasy here at Fonthill. He built a 12-ft high and 7-mile long wall around his estate to keep the world at bay and hired James Wyatt, one of the leading architects of the day. The first part built was the tower that reached about 300 ft before it collapsed. Beckford later said that he was sorry he did not see it fall himself. The replacement tower was finished six years later and collapsed as well. Beckford immediately started to build another one, this time with rock, and this work was finished in seven years. It was declared finished in 1813 and here Beckford lived his scandalous life with his household of young male servants until 1822, when his income from the sugar market collapsed. He was forced to sell Fonthill Abbey for £330,000 to an ammunitions dealer. The tower collapsed for the last time in 1825. The rest of the building was later demolished. Only the gatehouse and a small remnant of the north wing remain to this day. Beckford retired to Bath where he came to be regarded as respectably eccentric rather than seriously debauched, until his death in 1844 at the age of 84 with most of his fortune gone.

Walk 5

LANDFORD

*T*his very pleasant short walk makes an ideal expedition for a summer afternoon or a short winter day. It explores the parish of Landford on the northern edge of the New Forest and has delightful stretches of woodland walking linked by quiet field paths. A recurring theme is the river Blackwater and the route crosses and recrosses its several branches.

The Garden Room Café at Golden Acre Garden Centre is a very pleasant place to rest and be refreshed two-thirds of the way round the walk. There are some tables outside on a covered patio area overlooking the plants, as well as a spacious interior. There is a very good choice of cakes and gateaux, as well as cream teas, toasted teacakes and speciality ice creams. For lunch the options range from a choice of well presented sandwiches, through salads and ploughman's lunches to daily specials served between noon and 2.30 pm. It is open seven days a week between 9.30 am to 5 pm. Telephone: 01794 399808.

DISTANCE: 4 miles

MAP: OS Explorer 131 Romsey, Andover & the Test Valley and OL 22 New Forest

STARTING POINT: Cuckoo Inn, Hamptworth (GR 243196)

HOW TO GET THERE: From the A36, Salisbury–Southampton road, some 6 miles west of junction 2 of the M27, take the B3079 for 1/2 mile. Turn right on Hamptworth Road for 3/4 mile to an informal parking area on the left by a phone box and just before the Cuckoo Inn.

ALTERNATIVE STARTING POINT: If you wish to visit the teashop at the beginning or end of your walk, start at a lay-by on the A36 next to the Golden Acres Garden Centre containing the teashop. You will then start the walk at point 6.

THE WALK

1 Cross the road and take a signed footpath opposite. Follow the path diagonally right across three fields, through a small coppice and on in the same direction across a fourth field.

From this path there is a good view to the south across the New Forest, England's newest National Park designated in 2005. This part of the walk is within its boundary, which runs along the A36 round here.

2 Do not join the obvious track but turn left on a narrow path into a wood. (The sign is hidden in trees at the time of writing.) Follow this downhill to shortly reach a wooden bridge over the river Blackwater. There are many paths in this wood but the right of way is marked by yellow waymarks so watch for them. Over the bridge turn right for 130 yards, following the path round a sharp left-hand bend and ignoring a small bridge on the right. Immediately round the bend turn right on a smaller path, marked by a yellow arrow on a tree, and follow this to a second footbridge on the right across the river – a different branch.

3 Cross the footbridge into a tree nursery. Turn left for 30 yards, then right between the rows of trees, crossing a couple of tracks, to a stile onto a cross track.

4 Turn right along the track, with a wood on the left, for 100 yards then go over a stile on the left into the wood and follow the path through the trees to emerge on the track at the end. Cross the track and go ahead with a wire fence on the left to a stile and on to a major road, the A36.

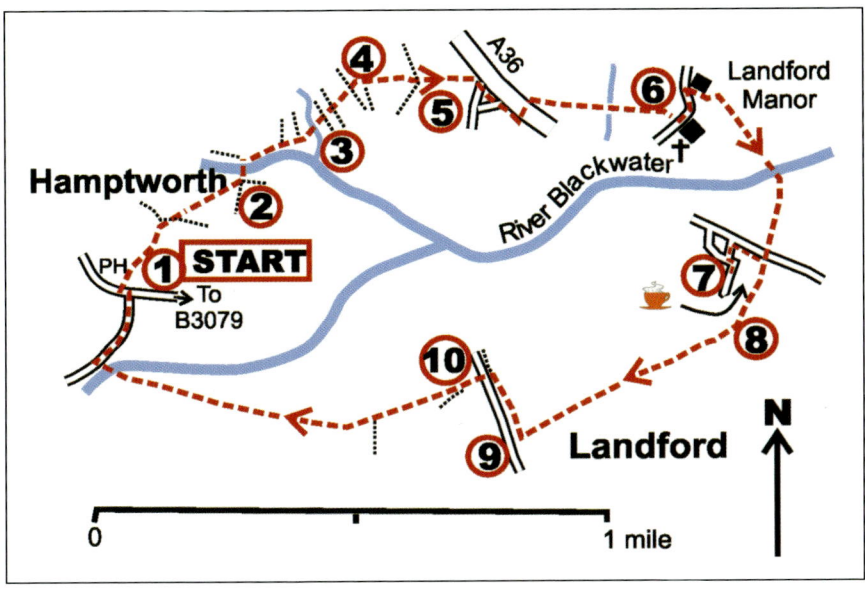

Landford is an ancient community and is mentioned in the Domesday Book. The parish seems never to have had an inn, although there was probably an unlicensed alehouse, until the Landford Poacher opened its doors in 1989. Much cider was made in Landford, perhaps because there was no pub, and a horse-drawn cider press toured farms and cottages to press the apples.

5 Turn right and cross the B3079 to walk alongside the A36. At the end of the footway, cross the road to a signed path starting up some steps to a stile. Over the stile, bear right to walk with a wire fence on the right. At the end of the field, go over a wooden footbridge and uphill across a second field, heading towards the church seen ahead, to a stile into a small field, which is the church car park, and cross this to a lane.

There has probably been a church here since Saxon times. It suffered terrible damage in a storm in 1689 when a great elm tree fell on the church. By 1856 it had become so dilapidated that it was deemed past repair and the present church was built, though some materials from the old structure were reused.

6 Turn left for 125 yards past Landford Manor, then turn right on a signed path along a track. Go to the right of farm buildings, then follow the track round to the left and then the right. When the track ends

Landford church, rebuilt in the 19th century.

at a stile by a field gate, continue ahead along the right-hand side of a narrow field to a footbridge to once again cross the river. Over the bridge, turn right and follow the path through a small farmyard back to the main road. Turn right to the teashop within Golden Acres Garden Centre.

7 From the teashop, turn right along the main road to return to the point where you joined the main road, then turn right on a hedged, signed path next to the entrance to Cherry Tree Farm. Follow the path to a second stile, into a field.

8 Turn right along the right-hand side of two fields and then along a track to a road.

9 Turn right along the footway for about 250 yards.

10 Turn left along a track, then shortly keep ahead, signed 'Restricted Byway'. Follow the track, eventually passing a ford across another branch of the river Blackwater, to a lane. Turn right back to the start.

Walk 6

OLD AND NEW SARUM

Old Sarum sits atop a natural hill and this commanding feature of the landscape was an important centre for nearly 5,000 years. Relatively recently, just under 800 years ago, the momentous decision was made to abandon the site and move to the valley below. Legend says the site of New Sarum or Salisbury is supposed to have been selected by firing an arrow from Old Sarum, clearly an impossibility given the distance involved, although it is sometimes claimed the arrow hit a white deer, which continued to run and died on the spot where the cathedral now stands. This walk starts at ancient Old Sarum and leads off the hill to a lovely riverside path right into the heart of the city. The return is on the opposite side of the valley at a higher level with some excellent views and an unexpectedly easy climb back to the start. Both Old and New Sarum are well worth taking the time to explore. Modern Salisbury is at the confluence of five rivers and the water meadows beside these are liable to flood. This means they have not been built on and so make a delightful traffic-free walking route.

Salisbury has a very wide choice of refreshment stops and the Polly Tea Rooms are ideally placed for this route just by the riverside path that takes you right into the city. Like its sister establishment in Marlborough (Walk 18), it is a charming and traditional teashop offering cream teas, with a choice of jam, or a selection of cakes, including several varieties of meringue. Possibilities for lunch include full meals such as wild boar sausages in a red wine and bean casserole or tempting lighter choices such as prawns in filo pastry with lemon and lime mayonnaise, as well as sandwiches or filled jacket potatoes. They also sell very tempting hand-made chocolates, though these are not the easiest things to carry if you do this walk in summer. There are some tables outside overlooking the square. Polly's is open until 5 pm every day. Telephone: 01722 336037.

DISTANCE: 5¹/₂ miles

MAP: OS Explorer 130 Salisbury & Stonehenge

STARTING POINT: Old Sarum car park (GR 139326). This is locked when the site closes at 6 pm in July and August, 5 pm in May, June and September, 4 pm in October and March and 3 pm in winter at the time of writing. If you think you might not make it back in time, start at the church in Stratford sub Castle (GR 130326), where there are several spots where a car can be left without causing inconvenience. Facing the church, turn right along the road to pick up the route at point 3.

HOW TO GET THERE: Old Sarum is close to and signed from the A345, Amesbury–Salisbury road, just north of Salisbury.

ALTERNATIVE STARTING POINT: If you wish to visit the teashop at the beginning or end of your walk, start in Salisbury using the Central long stay car park, which is on the route not far from the teashop. You will then pick up the walk at point 5.

THE WALK

1 Go over a stile to the left of the public conveniences and turn left along a bank beside a deep ditch. Walk round this to a path in a dip leading across the ditch.

This dry and windy site encompasses the grand sweep of British history, having been the site of a Neolithic settlement, an Iron-Age hill fort, a Roman military station, and a Norman palace and cathedral, before fading into history on a final sour note as a 'rotten borough'.

The Normans arrived shortly after their success at Hastings in 1066, fortified the hill and had built a timber castle before 1070, for it was already present

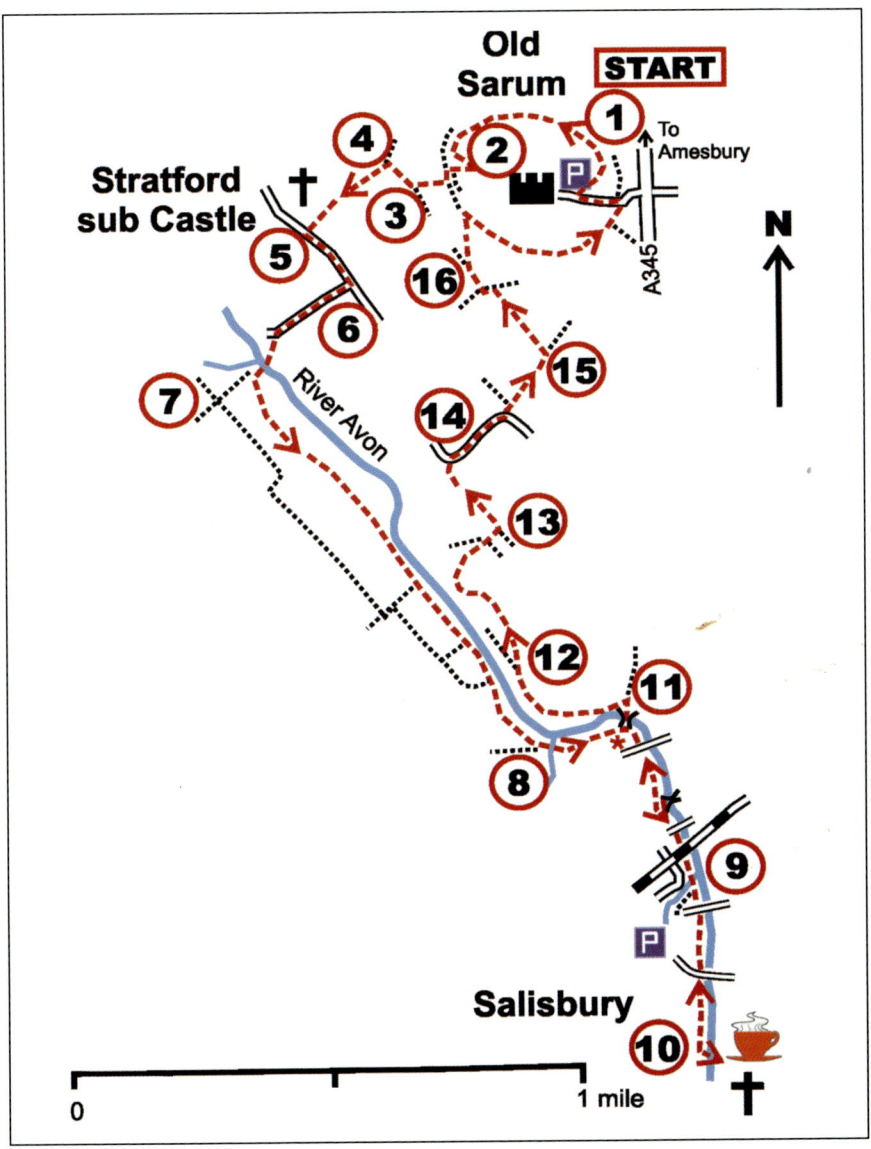

when William the Conqueror chose this location to pay off his troops and disband his army. Old Sarum was more than another Norman fortress, however; it was a royal castle, the property of the king. The king decreed that a cathedral should also be built at the castle, completed in 1092.

This first cathedral was hit by lightning and extensively damaged only five days after it was consecrated. Rather than repairing the building, the next bishop erected a replacement that was twice the size of the original, and that stood taller than the castle on the hill above it! Modelled on churches in Rome, the interior walls were covered in red porphyry and green marble, while the floor was made of slabs of white and green stone. There seems to have been constant conflict between castle and cathedral. The monks didn't enjoy having to rent dwellings from the soldiers, and since the soldiers controlled the gates, the monks complained that they often prevented worshippers from entering.

Eventually, by the 12th century, it was clear that the site was no longer suitable and the Pope was petitioned for permission to move the cathedral to a new site on water meadows 2 miles south.

2 Go down into the dip, then turn right across the ditch. On the far side, turn left for 30 yards, then fork right downhill to a T-junction.

3 Turn right to a surfaced track.

4 Turn left to a road in Stratford sub Castle.

5 Turn left.

6 Turn right along Mill Lane. At the end of the lane bear left on a surfaced path.

7 Immediately over a bridge across a branch of the river Avon, turn left over a stile and follow a permissive path across the water meadows and by

Old Sarum.

34

the river. Follow this delightful path for about a mile, heading towards the elegant spire of the cathedral leaping from the city at its base, to a T-junction with a cross path as the main river turns left.

Note: this is a permissive path that may be closed when cattle are grazing the water meadows and it can be very wet. In either case you can continue ahead for a further 90 yards to a cross path and turn left on an excellent fenced path. There are connections between these two paths at several points and they finally meet in a riverside park shortly before point 8.

New Sarum, or Salisbury, was founded in 1220. The main body of the cathedral was completed in only 38 years, using stones from the building at Old Sarum, and is a masterpiece of Early English architecture. At this time, cathedral construction was at the cutting edge of building technology, and errors of judgement led to the collapse of the central towers at both Winchester and Lincoln. With foundations only 4 ft deep and built on a gravel bed, Salisbury was lucky to escape this when the imposing spire was added 100 years later. However, the columns of the central crossing are now bowed by around ten inches.

8 Turn left to walk with the river Avon on the left to a footbridge across it. Note this point (*) but for now continue by the river. Cross a road and keep ahead on a paved cycleway beside the river.

9 When the cycleway and river both fork, near a large car park, bear left to keep the river on your left and shortly reach a road. Cross this and keep ahead, signed 'City Centre Cathedral', to shortly walk again by the river. Stay on the riverside walk until it goes under an arch. Do not walk beneath the arch but turn left, across the river, signed 'St Thomas's church', into St Thomas's Square and the teashop on the left next to the church.

10 Keep ahead if you wish to visit the cathedral. Otherwise, turn right out of the teashop back to the riverside path and retrace your steps to the footbridge over the river passed earlier in the walk (*). Note: If you started in Salisbury, the footbridge is in a park just as the river turns left.

11 Now turn right across the bridge. Immediately over the bridge turn left to again walk beside the river but now on the opposite bank. Follow this path for about ¼ mile to a fork.

⑫ Take the right branch, climbing slightly. Follow the main path along the top of a bank. Stay on the main path as it bears left for a few yards then turns right to eventually meet a paved cycleway.

⑬ Turn left to a road.

⑭ Turn right. When the road bends sharp right at Farthing Cottage, continue ahead on a track called 'The Portway' and keep ahead on a path when the track ends.

⑮ Watch for a large but not very obvious stone bearing an illegible plaque, on the left. Immediately after it, turn left through a gate. Walk along the left-hand side of a field. At the end of the field, go through a gate then left along a path for about 100 yards.

This sarcen stone marks the site of the Parliament Tree. Old Sarum was abandoned once New Sarum was built and there its history ended except for a footnote as the most notorious of the rotten boroughs. It had returned two MPs to Parliament since the time of Edward I and this continued despite the fact that few, if any, people actually lived there. The borough was a burgage franchise where the inhabitants of designated houses had the right to vote. From at least the 17th century it had no resident voters, but the overall landowner retained the right to nominate tenants for each of the burgages, who were not required to live there. In 1802, the Pitt family sold the borough for £60,000, even though the land and manorial rights were worth £700 a year at most, an indication of the value of a pair of Parliamentary seats. The elections actually took place on a hustings under a tree on the site of the stone memorial. Rotten boroughs were swept away by the Reform Act of 1832.

⑯ Go through a gate on the right and follow the path uphill to meet a cross path that contours round the hill. Turn right along this path, then left up the drive leading to the car park where this walk started.

This site has had many names through the centuries that evolved into the modern 'Salisbury'. Sarum, often thought to be the Roman or Norman name, is actually a medieval 'typo'. Documents were written in contracted Latin and it was easier to write Sar with a stroke over the 'r', than write the complete word 'Saresberie'. That mark of contraction was also the common symbol for the Latin termination 'um'. Hence, 'Sar' with a stroke over the 'r' was copied as 'Sarum'.

Walk 7

SHEAR WATER

*L*ongleat *is a well-known tourist destination but this route, partly within the estate, is far away from the stately house and safari park. Shear Water Lake is a haven for fishing and sailing and lies in a beautiful wooded section of the estate, which is explored on the walk. The central part is through more open countryside along the side of a hill with excellent views. The walk then re-enters the estate and passes through a plantation where there are some magnificent beeches among the conifers. The route ends round the edge of the lake and then through more very attractive woodland.*

The refreshment stop for this walk is one of the most unusual I have ever visited as it is a dual establishment. On one side is the Fisherman's Rest Café with wooden benches and tables outside and a menu designed for the eponymous anglers, comprising things with chips, generously filled sandwiches and mugs of tea. The Bargate Thatch Tearoom, by contrast, has wrought-iron furniture outside and lace tablecloths within.

Pots of tea are served with china cups, together with delicious cakes and scones. I thought the coffee and walnut cake I enjoyed was so light that I should hold it down between bites. So, you can take your choice of the style you prefer. They are both open daily in the summer and weekends and Tuesday and Thursday in winter. The Fisherman's Rest opens about 8 am for breakfast and the tearoom rather later. Telephone: 01985 213255.

There is no other source of refreshment when the teashop is closed.

DISTANCE: 6 miles

MAP: OS Explorer 143 Warminster & Trowbridge

STARTING POINT: Nockatt Coppice car park (GR 828423)

HOW TO GET THERE: From the A362 Frome–Warminster road, about ½ mile west of its junction with the A350 at a roundabout take a minor road south, signed 'Horningsham', for about a mile to a car park on the left.

ALTERNATIVE STARTING POINT: If you wish to visit the teashop at the beginning or end of your walk, start at Shear Water where there is ample parking in a car park across the road from the teashop (charge). You will then start the walk at point 7.

THE WALK

1 Facing the road, take a track on the right, next to a map board. After 50 yards follow the main track round to the right and continue on this path for about ½ mile.

2 When the main track turns sharp left, press on in the same direction on a somewhat smaller track and follow this to a lane.

3 Cross the lane to another lane a few yards to the right, signed 'Restricted Byway', going uphill to Shute Farm. Walk between buildings, then continue ahead on a track. When the fence on the left ends and the track fades, keep ahead along the right-hand side of three fields. At the end of the hedge on the right, keep ahead and soon a more distinct track develops. Follow this round a right-hand bend to reach a T-junction with a cross track almost immediately.

4 Turn left for 20 yards, then turn right on a grassy track and follow this to a main road, ignoring a track on the right.

5 Turn left along a footway. Stay on the footway as it diverges from the main road to reach a cul-de-sac and go ahead to a lane.

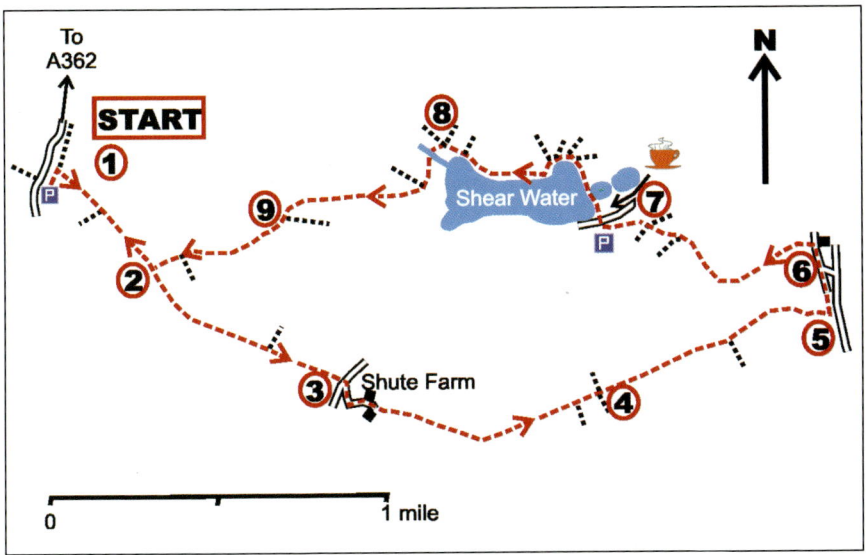

6 Turn left for 150 yards. At Foxholes House on the right turn left, signed 'Restricted Byway', on a rising path just inside a wood. Stay on the path as it bears round to the right, then bear right at a clear fork. Follow the path over a cross path and then bear left down to a car park. Cross the car park and lane to the teashop.

7 From the teashop, turn right to walk with the lake on the left. At the end of the lake, bear left to continue on a surfaced drive round the lake.

8 Take the first major track on the left, signed 'Nockatt Car Park' on a large stone. Follow this for about $^2/_3$ mile to a T-junction.

9 Turn right and press on to a second T-junction. Turn right and follow the lovely woodland track walked at the start of the route back to the car park.

(If you started at Shear Water, turn left at the second T-junction and when you reach a lane follow the directions from point 2.)

Walk 8

BRATTON

This walk encapsulates much of what Wiltshire has to offer the walker, with far-reaching views and relics of the distant past. It explores the downland between the forbidding isolation of Salisbury Plain and the vale to the north. The downland is rich in wild flowers in the summer and also home to many birds and insects, some of them rare, such as the Adonis Blue butterfly. The route descends the steep scarp slope to touch two of the villages strung out along its foot before climbing back to the start, the site of an Iron Age fort surrounding a much older Neolithic burial mound and home to one of Wiltshire's white horses.

The tearoom at Fitzroy Farm on the edge of Bratton is housed in old stable buildings and also has several tables on an extensive lawn in front. It serves cream teas and a good choice of cakes. There is a choice of fillings for sandwiches, jacket potatoes and salads and you are invited to choose your own combination. These are supplemented by daily specials. The Old Stable Tearoom is open every day throughout the year between 10 am and 4 pm. Telephone: 01380 831242.

DISTANCE: 6 miles

MAP: OS Explorer 143 Warminster & Trowbridge

STARTING POINT: White Horse car park near Westbury (GR 899513)

HOW TO GET THERE: From the B3098 on the east side of Westbury take a minor road, signed 'White Horse', to a car park at the top of the hill.

ALTERNATIVE STARTING POINT: If you wish to visit the teashop at the beginning or end of your walk, start at Fitzroy Farm. Permission should be sought before leaving a car for an extended period. You will then start the walk at point 6.

THE WALK

It is worth first exploring Bratton Camp, an Iron-Age hill fort enclosing a Neolithic barrow, and information boards explain what is to be seen. If you go right to the edge of the slope, you get a close-up view of the famous white horse and again, there is an interesting information point.

A prominent feature in the views from this walk, many would say a blot on the landscape, is the 400-ft high chimney of the Blue Circle cement works. This opened in the early 1960s exploiting locally quarried chalk. The works and quarry are now owned and operated by Lafarge. They employ about 130 people on the site and estimate that they contribute £10 million a year to the local economy. Not only do they produce cement, they also get rid of old tyres by burning them, which saves on fossil fuels and makes money. They also plan to burn recycled liquid fuel made from solvents used in the manufacturer of products like paint and nail varnish remover. Considerable fears have been raised locally about the nature and effects of the emissions this waste disposal operation generates.

1 Return to the access road and turn right. When the road bends left, turn right along a broad track to a T-junction with a cross track.

2 Turn left. Eventually this becomes a surfaced lane. Continue ahead to a T-junction.

An area of Salisbury Plain about the size of the Isle of Wight is under military control, and is used extensively for training purposes. Access by the public is extremely limited. This part, surrounding the village of Imber, was

Westbury's white horse.

41

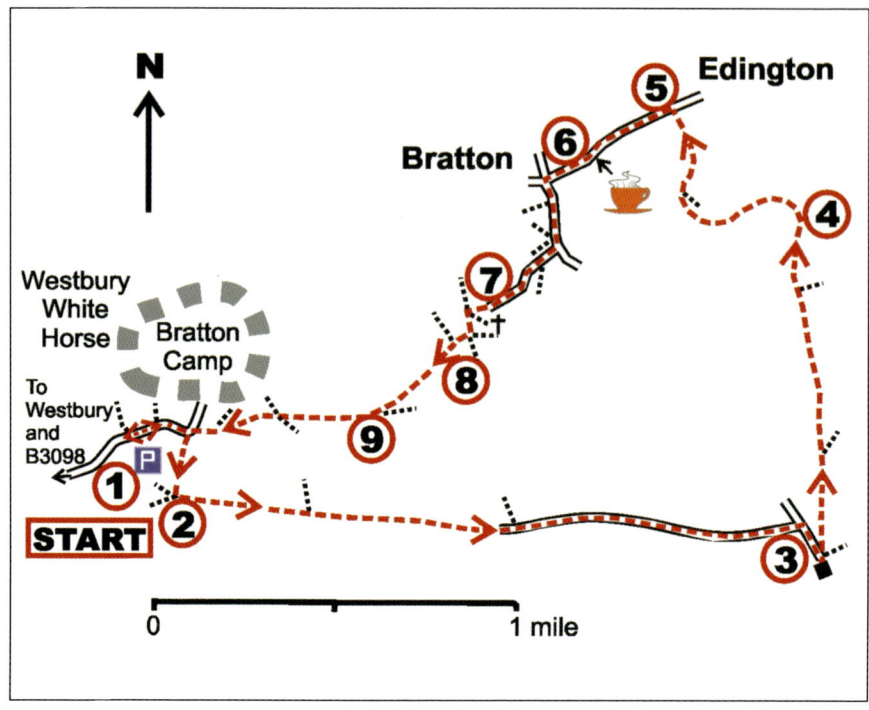

closed to the public and used for live firing during the Second World War, in 1943. The military bought parcels of land around Imber from the late 1920s onwards. Agriculture was depressed and the good prices offered by the military encouraged people to sell land, with few being put off by the conditions of their sale, which allowed the War Office to assume control and evict the residents if necessary. By the Second World War almost all of the land in and around Imber was owned by the military.

3 Turn right for 150 yards. At a guard post on the right, turn sharp left on an unsigned path. After about ¹/₄ mile bear left through a metal field gate and follow the path almost to the top of the hill.

4 Follow the path (and wire fence) round to the left and downhill and stay on this path to a road.

In the 9th century, the Danes had been steadily invading England, pushing ever further south and east. Their advance was halted by Alfred the Great. He mustered the Anglo-Saxon forces at Egbert's Stone, which may have been near Stourhead (see Walk 1). Battle was joined at Ethandun, which is thought to be Edington, in May AD 878. Alfred defeated the Danes and chased them back to Chippenham, where Alfred's forces laid siege for two weeks before the Danes surrendered and accepted peace terms. This battle marks the turning point in that attempt by the Vikings to conquer the British Isles. The Anglo Saxon people under King Alfred and his successors went on to bring together the kingdoms of England (Wessex, Anglia, Mercia and Northumbria) under one king and so, taking a rather romantic view, it may be said that the English nation started from this victory. There is a memorial sarcen stone near the car park where this walk started.

 ⑤ Turn left along the road to Fitzroy Farm and the teashop on the left.

⑥ Return to the road from the teashop and turn left into Bratton. Take the first road on the left, Stradbrook, signed 'St James church'. Bear right along Church Road to the church.

The present parish of Bratton is formed from several small early communities with the church belonging to one of these, Littlestoke, which has disappeared. It is possible that there was a Saxon church on this site and the present building dates mainly from the early 15th century. It is worth taking the time to visit to look at the interesting carvings such as the gargoyles on the tower. There is more information within.

⑦ Take a signed path to the right of the church, starting down some steps. Follow the path round the back of the church and up to a cross path with a metal kissing gate to the left. Turn right to soon reach another metal kissing gate.

⑧ Through the gate, bear left uphill following a line of trees. At the end of the trees look for a faint path rising diagonally up the slope in the same direction and follow this up the side of the combe to the top.

⑨ Turn right along the top of the combe. Go through a metal gate and continue in the same direction to a cross path with a metal gate on the right. Go through the gate and immediately over a stile on the left to continue in the same direction to a stile by a gate onto the car park access road (*) and keep ahead back to the car park.

(*If you started at Fitzroy Farm, turn left here.)

Walk 9

STONEHENGE

The world-famous stone circle at Stonehenge sits in a complex landscape produced by centuries of labour, producing burial mounds, enclosures and henges. This truly fascinating walk, which is well provided with information boards, explores its intriguing legacy, the oldest part dating back more than 5,000 years. The National Trust now owns the surrounding downs and is working with farmers to restore the chalk grassland with the result that there is a wonderful display of wild flowers, together with the associated butterflies and birds, to enjoy on parts of the walk in summer. The stones, a World Heritage Site, attract throngs of eager visitors from all over the world, but you are required to pay English Heritage a hefty fee to get anywhere near and you certainly aren't allowed within touching distance. On this walk, which is remarkably quiet away from the hoards round the monument, you can enjoy a glimpse of England's remote past, and get a good cup of tea part way round to refresh you for yet more enigmatic ancient remains in the second half.

Stonehenge Café sells a selection of cakes, sandwiches and baguettes, together with hot snacks. The appropriately-named Rock Cake is popular. It has several outside tables nearby and there are picnic tables around the site but there is no indoor accommodation. Stonehenge is open throughout the year. Telephone: 0870 3331181.

DISTANCE: 5$\frac{1}{2}$ miles
MAP: OS Explorer 130 Salisbury & Stonehenge
STARTING POINT: Woodhenge car park (GR 151436)
HOW TO GET THERE: Woodhenge is signed from the A345, Amesbury–Marlborough road, about $\frac{3}{4}$ mile north of its junction with the A303. Take a minor road to a small car park on the right as the road makes a sharp left turn.
ALTERNATIVE STARTING POINT: If you wish to visit the teashop at the beginning or end of your walk, start at Stonehenge where there is a large car park at the time of writing. The teashop is by the entrance to the monument. You will then start the walk at point 6.

THE WALK

Durrington Walls is clearly visible to the north from the car park. A massive circular earthwork, or henge, nearly one-third of a mile in diameter, it has been much damaged by ploughing and was cut through by the A345 but its tall banks can still be seen. It was built in the Neolithic period around 3100 to 2400 BC and was much larger than Avebury. Excavations have revealed two circular series of massive timber posts and vast quantities of animal bones, which could indicate that feasts took place here. Excavations have also uncovered a massive Neolithic roadway – the first of its kind in Europe – made of compacted chalk and leading down to the river Avon from the henge entrance. This has led to the theory that there was a ceremonial link between Durrington Walls and Stonehenge, which had The Avenue, visited later in the walk, also leading down to the river. Possibly the wooden structures at Durrington Walls, temporary and subject to decay, were representative of the land of the living, while the stones at Stonehenge, permanent and unchanging, represented the world of the ancestors. The remains of the newly deceased, it is hypothesised, were brought here, perhaps at the winter solstice when the year dies and is regenerated, to make a literal and metaphorical journey along these routes and the river into the afterlife.

1 Continue along the road past the Woodhenge site. Just past Woodhenge go through a wooden gate on the left and bear half right across a meadow to find a gate onto a hedged path. (Note: at the time of writing this is an unusual wire gate where you have to lift a handle to open it.)

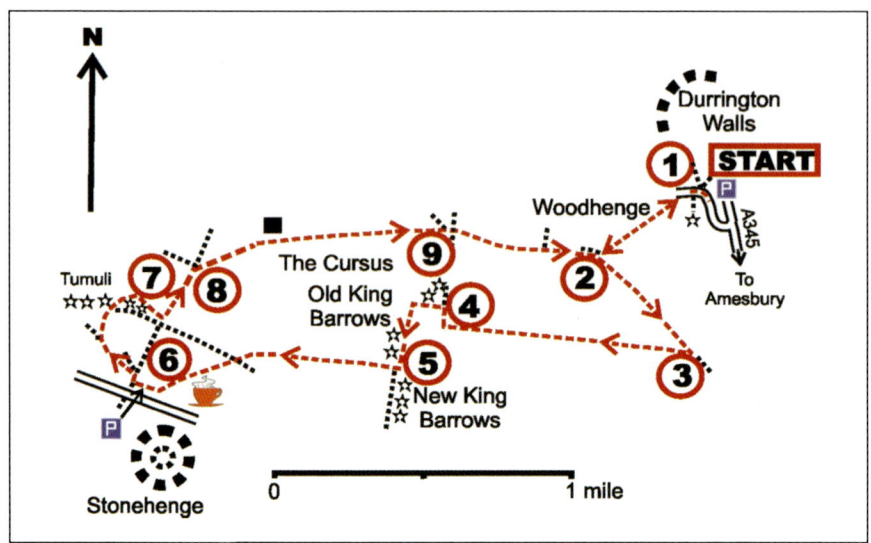

Before Stonehenge was built thousands of years ago, the whole of Salisbury Plain *was a forest of towering pines and hazel woodland. Over centuries the forest was cleared so the monument originally sat in more open chalk downland. In more recent times this was replaced by modern intensive agriculture, some of which can still be seen. The National Trust now owns much of the land round Stonehenge and is working with farmers to restore the traditional chalk grassland with a wonderful display of wildflowers, as in this meadow, in summer.*

2 Turn left along the path for about ½ mile.

3 Go through a gap in the hedge on the right, onto a track, and turn right, signed 'Old King Barrows'. This eventually goes round a sharp right bend to a junction marked by a fingerpost.

4 Turn left, signed 'King Barrows'. Follow the track round to the left to a small wooden gate on the right just before a second information board.

From this path it is clear why there is so much argument about the setting of Stonehenge in the 21st century. Your eye is drawn to the jumble of the car park or the traffic on the nearby A303 and you have to search out the stones beyond. There have been ambitious schemes to resite the visitor facilities to attempt to restore some tranquillity to the site but these depend on road improvements so everything is still under discussion at the time of writing. There is one school of

The famous stones.

thought that says this is merely another chapter in the long history of Stonehenge and that cleaning up the landscape would be just another form of inauthenticity.

5 Turn right through the gate. This is the course of The Avenue and is not visible on the ground at the time of writing. Head in the direction of a gap in woods, where the silhouette of a bank can be seen on the skyline, down into a valley to find a small wooden gate. Through the gate, go ahead to an information board. About here The Avenue turned left up to Stonehenge but we make our way to a car park seen ahead to a gate towards the left-hand end. The teashop is in the car park by the entrance kiosk to the monument.

6 Leaving the teashop, make your way to the far end of the surfaced car park to find a track. Turn right for 30 yards, then turn left through a small wooden gate. Follow the path ahead to one group of three and one group of two barrows. Go round behind the group of two to an information board, then bear right to a gate onto a track by yet another information board.

7 Turn left.

8 Some 35 yards after an information board on the left about The Cursus, go over a stile on the right and bear slightly left towards a small building to a stile by a field gate. Now keep ahead with a fence on the left.

9 At the end of a long field join a track. When the track turns right, continue ahead on a fenced path. Follow the path as it bears round to the right and watch for the point where you joined the path about 50 yards after passing under power cables. Go left up the embankment to the wire gate and head back across the meadow to the start.

(Continue along the path, if you started at Stonehenge.)

47

Walk 10

BRADFORD-ON-AVON
AND AVONCLIFF

*T*his walk packs huge variety into its few miles. Starting by an interesting building of considerable historic interest, it has quiet field paths from which there are superb views, shady woodland, a canal towpath with the interest of the canal traffic, and riverside walking. These excellent views have to be 'bought', of course, and the height is gained by a short, sharp climb up a lane out of Bradford-on-Avon. It must be admitted that this is something of a slog but it is not long and well worth it for the vistas from the ridge. This section is followed by the complete contrast of woodland rich in ferns that leads to Avoncliff, where the Kennet and Avon Canal crosses the river Avon. The return is easy level walking, partly by the canal and partly by the river.

The Mad Hatter at Avoncliff is a delightful place to sit and take in the scenery as it is in a wonderful position beside the aqueduct and has extensive gardens. For less clement weather there are a few tables indoors. They serve cream teas and tempting cakes cut in very generous slices. For lunch there is a choice of sandwiches, filled jacket potatoes and salads supplemented by daily specials and an all-day breakfast. The Mad Hatter is open every day throughout the year from 10.30 am until 6 pm in the winter and into the evening in summer. Telephone: 01225 868123.

DISTANCE: 3$^{1}/_{2}$ miles
MAP: OS Explorer 156 Chippenham & Bradford-on-Avon
STARTING POINT: Barton Farm Country Park car park (charge) (GR 823604)
HOW TO GET THERE: Follow the signs from the southern end of Bradford on Avon.
ALTERNATIVE STARTING POINT: If you wish to visit the teashop at the beginning or end of your walk, start in Avoncliff where there is a car park just before the end of the road. The teashop is next to the car park. You will then start the walk at point 7.

THE WALK

1 Take the path from the car park to the tithe barn.

Walk past the barn on the left to a T-junction. Turn left up some steps to the Kennet and Avon canal and turn left along the towpath, signed 'Bradford Lock', until it joins a road.

Medieval nuns certainly built to last! This impressive barn has been standing since the 14th century, when it was built by Shaftesbury Abbey, the richest nunnery in England. Although called the Tithe Barn, it was actually part of the abbey's farm or grange here and stored the produce of the abbey's own lands. One of the largest and best preserved of its kind in England, the barn is 167 ft long and 30 ft wide. Huge timbers support a massive roof made up of 30,000 stone tiles. The barn is now owned by English Heritage and is open every day (free) between 10.30 am and 4 pm.

2 Turn right on the road over a bridge. Immediately over the bridge, turn right again and follow the lane uphill.

3 Some 70 yards after a road on the left called 'Southleigh', take a footpath on the left starting over a stile by a gate. Head across the field to find a stile at the far end. Continue in the same direction along the right-hand side of three small fields. In the fourth field, with a communications mast on the right, head slightly left to find a stile next to a metal water trough. Now press on along the left-hand side of the next field and some 85

49

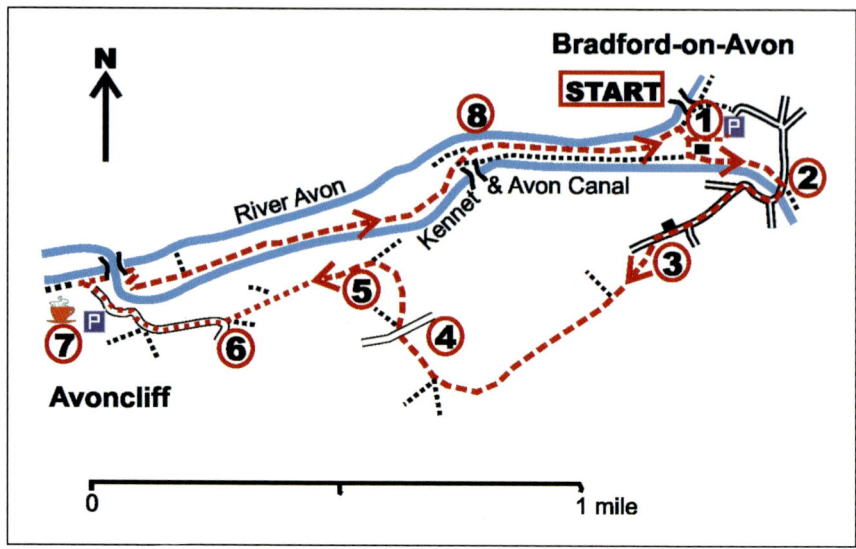

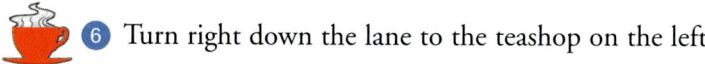

yards of the following one to two stiles on the left. Do not cross either of them but bear slightly right across the field to a stile onto a lane.

④ Cross the lane and take the right-hand one of two tracks. After 20 yards, go through a gate on the right into a field where a view of Bradford-on-Avon and the Avon valley opens up. Walk along the left-hand side of two fields, then bear right, downhill, to a stile. Over this stile, contour round and slightly down the hillside to a metal kissing gate into woodland.

⑤ Follow the main path, initially just inside the wood. At a fence corner on the right follow the main path as it bears left uphill into the wood and follow this to a lane.

⑥ Turn right down the lane to the teashop on the left.

⑦ From the teashop, turn left down the lane, right under the aqueduct, then right again up to the canal towpath. Turn left, signed 'Bradford-on-Avon Country Park'.

This is the Kennet and Avon canal (see Walk 12). Work here at Avoncliff was started in 1796 to build this 110-yard long aqueduct to carry the canal over the river Avon. It is built of Bath stone and was finished in 1798. It consists of

The aqueduct over the river Avon.

three arches – a central elliptical arch of 60 ft span with two side arches, each semicircular and 34 ft across. The central arch sagged immediately after the structure was finished. When restoration work started at the end of the 20th century it turned out that it had been built with faulty stone that had come from the canal company's own quarry midway between Limpley Stoke and Avoncliff and it had not stood the test of time well. However, all the problems were overcome and the canal is now busy with pleasure boats.

8 At a bridge across the canal, bear left away from the canal down a surfaced path to pick up a riverside path and continue in the same direction to the tithe barn and the start. (You can, of course, continue by the canal to the point where you joined it, if you wish.)

Bradford-on-Avon is a particularly delightful town to explore, with much of interest to see, including a 7th-century church, the town bridge complete with lock-up, and a wealth of attractive buildings. To walk into the town, continue along the path by the river. Maps and more information are available from the tourist information centre.

Walk 11

URCHFONT

*T*his walk starts by climbing steadily up to Salisbury Plain. The ascent is not arduous and is rewarded with spectacular views across the Vale of Pewsey on one side and Salisbury Plain on the other. After a mile or so along the top of the steep scarp slope the route descends into the vale. The return leg is a complete contrast, using field paths to potter from one village to the next, with an abundance of thatched cottages and passing a farm shop with a tearoom before returning to Urchfont. All in all, this is a very attractive and varied walk that catches the essence of Wiltshire. Do this walk at the end of April or the beginning of May and you see some strange beings that swell the population around that time …

Mipo at Home at Plank's Farm Shop offers a good range of cakes such as, on my visit, a delicious and unusual apricot and almond fruit loaf. For lunch there is a selection of sandwiches, extending from what they refer to as 'basic butties' such as cheese and tomato to 'sumptuous sarnies' such as Brie, bacon and cranberry with orange relish. There is also a choice of salads and quiche and daily specials. There are some tables outside in an attractive courtyard. Mipo is open Monday to Saturday between 10 am and 5 pm and Sunday until 4 pm from Easter to October. Telephone: 01380 840909.

> **DISTANCE:** 6½ miles
> **MAP:** OS Explorer 130 Salisbury & Stonehenge
> **STARTING POINT:** Informal parking area at Stonepit Lane, Urchfont (GR 040568)
> **HOW TO GET THERE:** The starting point is on the B3098 that links the A342 and A360 via Urchfont and Market Lavington. The parking area is at the south-west side of the village. If this is full, there are other spots round Urchfont where a car may be left without causing inconvenience.
> **ALTERNATIVE STARTING POINT:** If you wish to visit the teashop at the beginning or end of your walk, start at Plank's Farm Shop, though permission should be sought before leaving a car for an extended period. You will then start the walk at point 11.

THE WALK

In 1932 a writer claimed to have found the name of this village spelled in no fewer than 65 ways, including forms with each of the five vowels as the initial letter. By 2001 the tally was 111 spellings using ten different initial letters – such changeability must surely be unique. The name probably means 'spring of Eohric'.

1 Take a path leading from the pull-off (not the surfaced path to houses). After passing beneath pylons, the view opens out: press on along the path up the hill and follow round to the right to meet a major track some 40 yards after the bend.

2 Turn left along the track to reach another track at a junction of tracks and bridleway.

3 Turn left and walk along the track for about 1½ miles, keeping ahead at Redhorn Vedette.

To the right of the track are views across Salisbury Plain. About half the plain is given over to military training (see Walk 8). The Royal School of Artillery is based at Larkhill not far from here, and live firing is conducted on the plain for approximately 340 days of each year, as you may be aware by the sounds.

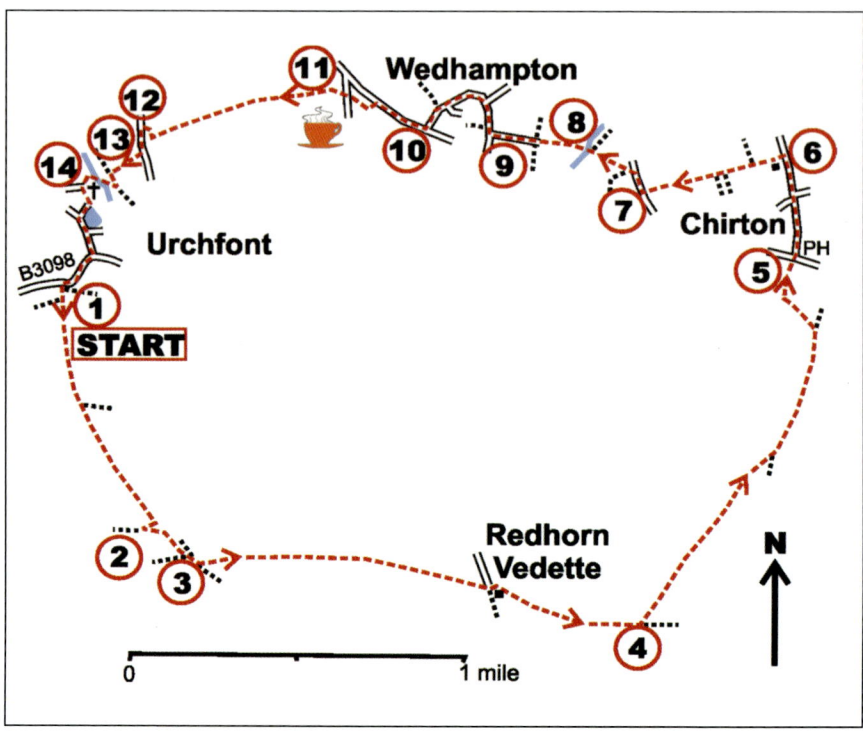

4 Take an unsigned path on the left. This is opposite a sign warning the public about the danger from unexploded shells and mortar bombs and about ¹/₂ mile after Redhorn Vedette. Follow the main path down to a main road.

5 Cross the road and continue ahead on a minor road called 'The Hollow' into Chirton.

Chirton, like Urchfont, is typical of the many villages that lie along the foot of the steep slope and has been here since at least Saxon times, the name being a corruption of the Saxon 'Cherrington', meaning 'the farm by the church'. The reason there is this string of villages along the foot of the steep scarp slope is that springs emerge at the bottom of the slope, so there was always a ready supply of water.

6 Just after Manor Farm turn left, signed 'Footpath to Conock'. Follow first a surfaced path and then a track, passing an unexpected statue, to a lane.

7 Turn right for 130 yards. As you approach the gates of Conock Old Manor, turn left on a track for 10 yards then turn right through a kissing gate next to a field gate. Go across the field to a metal kissing gate then continue ahead, over a footbridge, into a second field.

8 Turn left to walk along the left-hand side of the field. Cross a track and continue ahead to a T-junction with a lane in Wedhampton.

9 Turn right and follow the lane through the village, bearing left on Greengate Road at a junction, to a main road.

10 Turn right for about 300 yards. At a brown tourist sign, turn left to a surfaced track and follow this to a lane and the entrance to Plank's Farm Shop and the teashop.

11 From the teashop, return to the parking area and turn left on a signed path. At the time of writing this rather gets lost in farm clutter at the rear of the farm but make your way through this to pick up the path again, leading in the direction shown on the sign by the car park. The path is not very obvious on the ground but goes in more or less a straight line to reach a gap in a hedge. It then goes across a field to a stile and along the left-hand side of the next field to a lane.

12 Turn left for about 130 yards. More or less opposite a thatched garage, turn right through a wooden kissing gate on a signed path to walk along the left-hand side of a field to a kissing gate into a wood.

13 At a T-junction a few yards into the wood, turn left downhill to shortly reach a second, larger T-junction. Turn right and follow the path up out of the valley to emerge by a church.

14 Go ahead for 60 yards, then turn left up steps on a path by the church leading to the village pond. Press on by the pond and along the village street to a main road. Turn right back to the start.

As the May Bank Holiday looms, strange beings start appearing all over the village. Urchfont Scarecrow Festival was started in 1997 as an event to raise money for the refurbishment of the village hall. Following the success of the first year, the festival has become an annual event with 50 or so scarecrows illustrating the theme chosen for the year. The money raised from programmes, teas and the associated popular plant sale has supported all sorts of community ventures and organisations.

Walk 12

DEVIZES AND CAEN HILL LOCKS

Devizes exudes civic pride and it has every right to do so as it is a gracious and attractive town. This interesting walk starts by the Kennet and Avon canal where former wharf buildings have been turned into a museum and theatre. The route leads through the town and the town trail guide, available from the Tourist Information Office passed in Market Place, is worth acquiring for its wealth of information about the many historic buildings that can be seen. After leaving Devizes, the way circumnavigates part of the old castle park, with surprisingly good views, before diverting to the foot of a triumph of early 19th-century waterway engineering – Caen Hill Lock Flight. The teashop sits welcomingly at the top and the return leg leads by the canal back to the start.

Caen Hill Café is by the canal at the top of a long flight of locks and has wonderful views both from inside and from the garden where there are several tables. It is located in a building that was once a lock-keeper's cottage. It serves a good selection of cakes, as well as sandwiches, filled jacket potatoes and imaginative salad bowls such as brie and red grape. In winter this fare is supplemented by hot specials. It is open every day between Easter and the end of October between 10 am and 5 pm, lunch being served until 3 pm. In winter it closes at 3.30 pm and is shut on Monday and Tuesday. Telephone 01389 724880.

When the teashop is closed, the Black Horse pub overlooking the canal serves food and there are numerous options in Devizes.

DISTANCE: 5^1/$_2$ miles

MAP: OS Explorer 157 Marlborough & Savernake Forest and 156 Chippenham & Bradford-on-Avon

STARTING POINT: Wharf car park, Devizes (charge) (GR 404617)

HOW TO GET THERE: The car park lies off, and is signed from, the A361 on the north side of the town centre, by the Kennet and Avon canal.

ALTERNATIVE STARTING POINT: If you wish to visit the teashop at the beginning or end of your walk, start at the car park for Caen Hill Locks (charge), signed from the road to Rowde, which is off the A361 about 1^1/$_2$ miles west of Devizes. A track leads from the car park to the canal and teashop. You will then start the walk at point 8.

THE WALK

The Kennet and Avon canal is made up of three waterways. To the west, the Avon Navigation links Bristol and Bath, while in the east the Kennet Navigation runs between Newbury and the river Thames at Reading. The section in the middle is an artificial cut between Bath and Newbury. All three were owned by the Kennet and Avon Company and operated as one commercial enterprise between opening in 1810 and a hostile takeover by the Great Western Railway in 1852. Canal traffic was already in decline due to competition from the railway and this trend accelerated in the second half of the 19th century. By 1955 the canal was in a very poor condition and plans were made to abandon it, but it was brought back from the brink by the efforts of enthusiasts and over 40 years of restoration were completed in 2002. The museum tells the story of the building, operation, decline and restoration of the canal and is open between 10 am and 4 pm from March to Christmas. Telephone: 01380 721279.

1 Facing the canal and theatre, leave the car park by a path on the right, signed 'Market Place', that passes to the right of the museum building. At a road, turn right along Couch Street. Cross a main road and continue ahead along Snuff Street into Market Place.

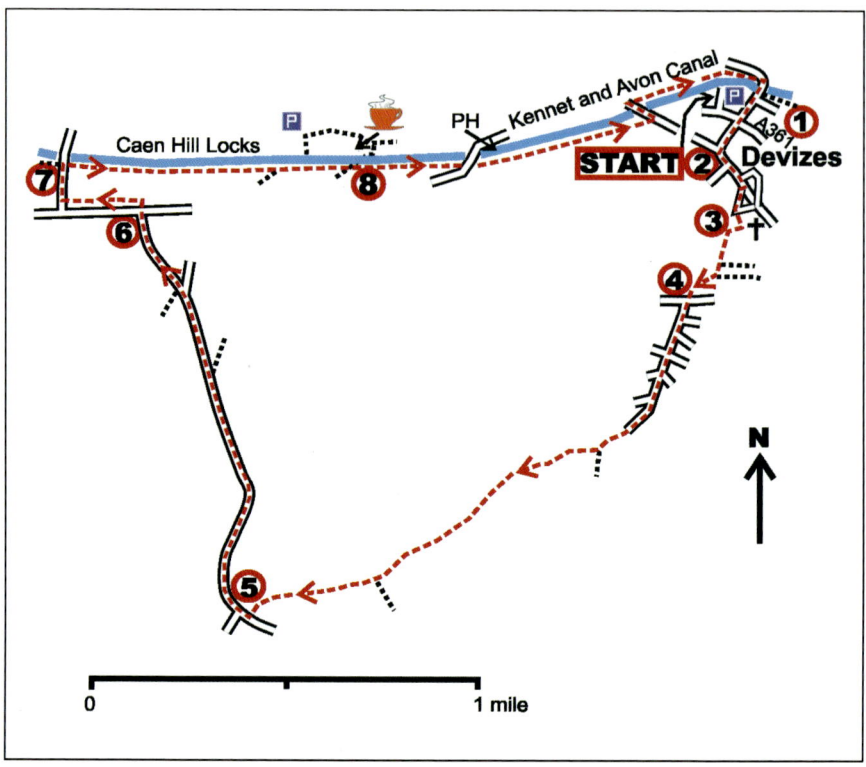

2 Turn left and walk along the right-hand side of Market Place, passing the Bear Hotel, then continue along St John's Street. Bear right at the town hall to St John's church.

The name Devizes derives from the Latin ad divisas, *which means 'at the boundaries', as the Norman bishop Osmund, nephew of William the Conqueror, built a castle here in about 1080 between the lands of two manors. A thriving medieval town developed and is a textbook example of medieval town planning. It doesn't look very medieval today because many of the buildings date from the time of Devizes' greatest prosperity when it was an important stop on the coach road to Bath and later from the trade brought by the canal. Have a look at the market cross, inscribed with the story of what happened to Ruth Pierce, a dishonest market trader, in 1753.*

3 Just inside the churchyard, turn right on a surfaced path that leads to a road.

You can glimpse the castle from this path. The original timber structure burned down and a stone castle was then constructed, which was thought to be one of the finest in Europe. This lasted until the Civil War, when it was demolished. The site was cleared and robbed of its remaining stone and windmills were built on the former motte. What we see today is a Victorian fantasy built in the second half of the 19th century and in private hands.

4 Cross the road and keep ahead along Hartmoor Road. Press on as this narrows to first a deeply sunken lane and then becomes a track to eventually reach a lane.

This was once an important approach to Devizes from the south and passes along the southern edge of what used to be a park associated with the castle. The lane used for the next part of the route was its western edge and the A361 was the northern boundary.

5 Turn right and walk along the lane to a main road.

6 Turn left, signed 'Trowbridge', crossing the road to make use of the footway on the right-hand side. Take the first right, signed 'Rowde', to the canal.

7 Immediately before the bridge over the canal, bear left off the road to the canal towpath. Turn right by the canal and climb up beside the locks of Caen Hill Flight to the teashop at the top.

Though Caen Hill is an undoubted engineering triumph, there is a whiff of scandal about the fact that it was built at all. In 1790 a young engineer, John Rennie, was commissioned to survey a route for the proposed canal and he opted for a more northerly route through Calne and Marlborough because it offered gradual changes in height and a more reliable water supply. His proposal was challenged by the chief engineer, Robert Whitworth. In 1793 the funds were in place to start work and Rennie was asked to undertake a second survey but it was to be submitted via Robert Whitworth. This time Rennie came up with the answer Whitworth wanted, despite the need to construct this dramatic flight of locks to accommodate the plunge of 237 ft in 2 1/2 miles from the western edge of the Vale of Pewsey at Devizes to the Avon valley. This route also called for a 4,312-yard long tunnel between Pewsey and Great Bedwyn. In addition, water supplies have always been a problem (see Walk 16). We do not know why Rennie changed his mind or why Whitworth was so set on the Devizes route, but it certainly helped trade in Devizes.

The Caen Hill flight of locks.

Caen Hill Flight was the last stretch of the Kennet and Avon canal to be finished and a horse-drawn tramway carried goods between the two sections until it was complete. When canal traffic was at its height, the locks were lit by gas lights and it must have been a dramatic sight. Each barge that passed through during the hours of darkness was charged a shilling.

8 Return to the canal towpath and turn left to continue by the canal. At the second road bridge go up some steps to the road, cross the road, then continue by the canal, signed 'Devizes Wharf', now on the opposite bank. At the next bridge, follow the path up to the road and turn right over the canal, then right again into the car park. (Keep ahead if you started at Caen Hill.)

Outside Wiltshire, Devizes is perhaps best known as the home of Wadworth's Brewery, founded in 1875 and still brewing in the town. They have a free visitor centre in New Park Street, a couple of minutes' walk from Market Place, which includes a tour of the brewery. Telephone: 01380 732277.

Walk 13

VALE OF PEWSEY

This easy walk explores the beautiful Vale of Pewsey and is a must for nature lovers. In its few short miles, it visits two contrasting nature reserves. One, on the first half of the walk, hosts a wonderful display of wild flowers in season. This is followed by a stretch beside the Kennet and Avon canal, with more wild flowers and birds, before tea overlooking the water. The last mile has an unavoidable few hundreds yards along a main road, redeemed by the benison of a footway followed by an idyllic woodland path through the second nature reserve and beside the river Avon.

The Waterfront is housed in old wharf buildings and is a double establishment with a pub above and bistro beneath. The latter has all the attributes of a very pleasant teashop, including a garden overlooking the canal and a good selection of tempting cakes. All-day breakfast is served, including the mighty Stonehenge that includes the absolute works. Possibilities for lunch include excellent sandwiches, filled jacket potatoes and main meals such as home-made salmon fishcakes. It is open every day between 8.30 am and 5 pm, just closing on Monday in winter. Telephone: 01672 564020.

DISTANCE: 4 miles

MAP: OS Explorer 157 Marlborough & Savernake Forest

STARTING POINT: Hallgate House car park, Broomcroft Road, Pewsey. (GR 164602)

HOW TO GET THERE: The car park is signed from the A345, Pewsey–Marlborough road, on the northern edge of Pewsey between the village and the station.

ALTERNATIVE STARTING POINT: If you wish to visit the teashop at the beginning or end of your walk, start at Pewsey Wharf where there is a public car park (charge). The teashop is next to the car park. You will then start the walk at point 8.

THE WALK

1 Facing the entrance to the car park, take a path on the left between houses to the main road. Turn left to walk into Pewsey. At the statue of King Alfred, turn left again, signed 'Burbage Milton Lilbourne'.

Originally there would have been a marshy island here formed by branches of the river Avon coming down the Vale from the north and east. The name of this community derives from the Saxon Pefisigge, meaning 'Pev's island'. King Alfred was crowned King of Wessex in AD 870 and owned much of the land in the Pewsey Vale. Legend has it that Alfred went off to war and left his wife in the care of the village. Upon his safe return, he granted the inhabitants of Pewsey the right to an annual feast, now incorporated into the modern-day carnival.

2 Some 25 yards after the Moonrakers pub, turn left on a signed path along a track called Brunkard's Lane. When this ends, keep on in the same direction along a road. Bear right along Martinsell Green when the road forks, then, at Scotchel Green, bear slightly right to pick up a fenced path again, starting down three shallow steps. Cross a road and continue ahead through a gate next to a field gate to reach the railway line. Do not turn right but cross the line and walk along the right-hand side of a field towards some thatched cottages.

3 In front of the cottages, turn right and this almost immediately becomes a lane. When the lane bends right at Highbanks, turn left on a public bridleway called Quiet Lane for 130 yards.

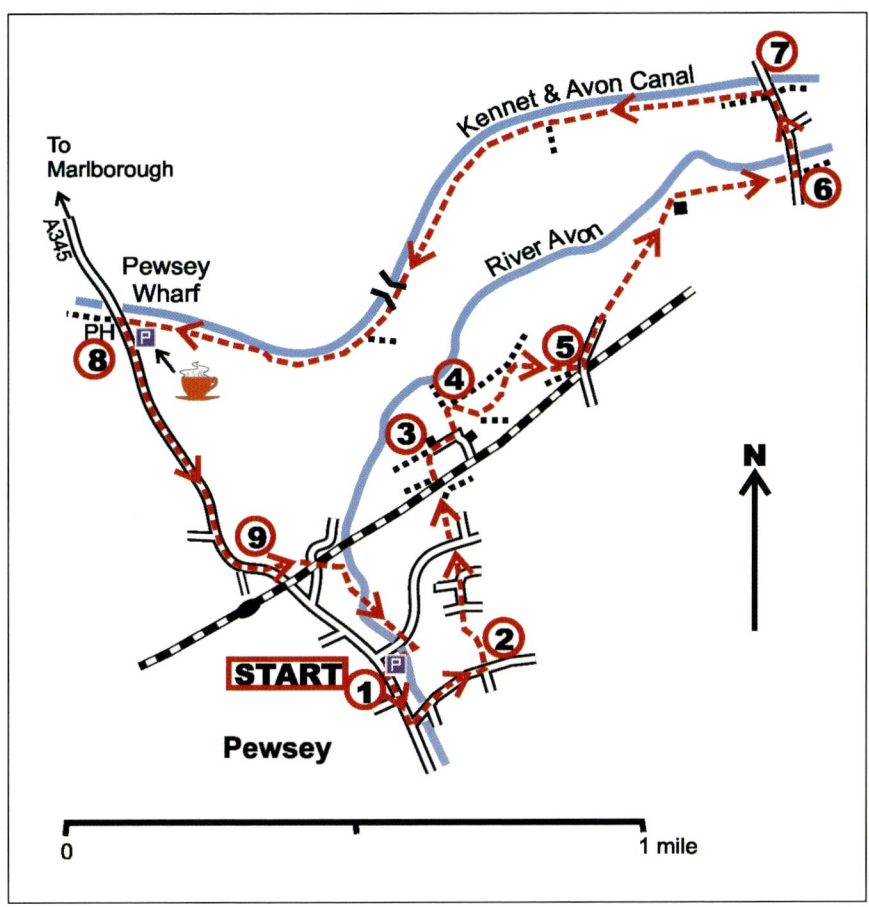

4 Take an unsigned path on the right that leads up steps and through a kissing gate into a meadow, part of Jones's Mill Nature Reserve. Through the gate, bear right immediately up to another kissing gate. Through this gate, turn left to walk with a fence on the left as far as a gate. At the gate turn right across the field to a gate onto a tiny lane and a seat strategically placed to enjoy the charming pastoral view.

5 Turn left along the lane. Continue ahead when this becomes the drive to Anvills Farm. As you approach the farm, leave the drive and go through a gate on the left to carry on walking beside the drive, past the farm. Follow the path round to the right to a lane.

The towpath of the Kennet and Avon canal.

6 Turn left towards a bridge over the Kennet and Avon canal.

For more information about the Kennet and Avon canal, see Walk 12.

 7 Immediately before the bridge, go through a gate on the right down to the towpath. Turn left beside the canal and walk along the canal for $1^1/_4$ miles to Pewsey Wharf and the teashop.

The Kennet and Avon canal had many wharves such as this along its length. It is believed locally that French prisoners of war worked on building the canal. At the end of their working day a horn called them back to their prison. This is thought to be the origin of the name of the pub across the road, the French Horn.

8 Turn left out of the teashop to the main road and turn left along the road.

9 Shortly after a road on the right to the station and before walking underneath the railway bridge, turn left on a path signed 'To Pewsey' and intriguingly called Way's Way. At a T-junction, turn right under the railway then turn left on a track. Follow the path through Scotchel Nature Reserve to a road. Cross the road and go ahead a few yards by the river to a bridge back to the car park.

Walk 14

LACOCK

*T*his pleasant walk exploring the countryside round Lacock is ideal for dawdling through a summer afternoon or as an invigorating outing for a short winter day. The village itself is undoubtedly one of Wiltshire's gems and well worth taking the time to explore and this walk, combined with a visit to Lacock Abbey and the associated Fox-Talbot Museum, makes a varied and interesting day's outing. The route uses lanes, footpaths and a surfaced cycleway and is easy going. It does climb a few feet and this miniscule effort is rewarded with some attractive views. One word of warning, however: it can be muddy after wet weather so suitable footwear makes the going more comfortable.

King John's Hunting Lodge is reputedly the oldest house in Lacock. The main part of the lodge dates back to the 13th century and still has much of the original cruck beam structure, whilst the rear of the building was added in Tudor times. In the 21st century it houses a charming traditional tearoom complemented by tables in the delightful garden complete with well-tended herbaceous borders. If you are really indulgent, you will enjoy King John's Royal Tea of smoked salmon sandwiches and scones with clotted cream, rounded off with dainty cakes. If that is a little too much, a cream tea, served with two sorts of jam and both white and wholemeal scones, is delicious. There is also a choice of tempting cakes. For lunch a range of sandwiches is offered, as well as light meals such as Wiltshire rarebit with red onion relish or spinach roulade with roasted peppers. The tearoom is open every day except Monday (open Bank Holidays) between 11 am and 5.30 pm. Telephone: 01249 730313.

DISTANCE: 3¹/₂ miles

MAP: OS Explorer 156 Chippenham & Bradford-on-Avon

STARTING POINT: National Trust car park for Lacock (charge for non-members) (GR 918682)

HOW TO GET THERE: Lacock and the car park are signed from the A350, Chippenham–Melksham road, about 3 miles south of Chippenham.

ALTERNATIVE STARTING POINT: Parking in Lacock is restricted so there is no other realistic starting place. If you wish to visit the teashop before the walk, make your way to the church and the teashop is next door.

THE WALK

1 Return to the road and turn right, then right again at a junction. Walk along the road for about ³/₄ mile to a road on the right called Forest Lane. Continue along the road for a further 65 yards.

The building seen to the left is Lacock Abbey, founded in 1229 by Ela, Countess of Salisbury, in memory of her husband. After the Dissolution in 1539, William Sharrington, who had made a fortune as Vice Treasurer of the Mint in Bristol through reducing coin sizes and pocketing the difference, acquired the abbey for £763. Later the abbey fell, literally if the romantic story is to be believed, into the hands of the Talbot family. It is said the heiress to the estate was in love with John Talbot but her father disapproved and locked her in the tower. She leapt from the window into her lover's arms, whereupon her father relented and allowed her to marry him. The house remained in the Talbot family until it was given to the National Trust in 1944.

2 Turn left along a track across Bewley Common. After 90 yards, bear half right on a path across the common to meet another track. Turn left. When the track ends at a house, continue ahead to the right of the building to a gate and stile into a field.

The two little gatehouses overlooking Bewley Common are nicknamed 'Night & Day' and are the western entry to Bowden Park estate. In years past, an old couple

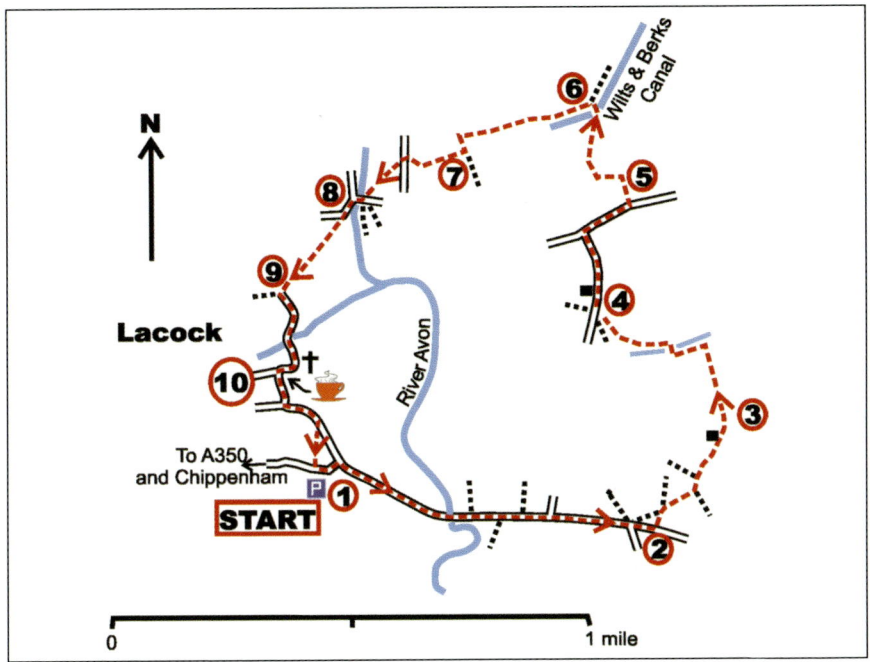

used to live in them, using one for a living room and the other for a bedroom, travelling from one to the other every morning and then back again in the evening.

③ Walk across the field, heading towards the left-hand corner of a wood on the opposite side, then keep ahead to the corner of the field. Turn left along the edge of the field. About halfway along, turn right down some steps, and cross a plank bridge over a stream and a stile into another field. Turn left round the edge of the field to an obscure stile about 100 yards after a gate on the left onto a lane by some cottages. (Note: the OS map shows these paths leading across the fields but as is often the case when fields are under arable cultivation, the path lies round the edge at the time of writing.)

④ Turn right to a T-junction. Turn right again for 180 yards.

⑤ Turn left on a surfaced path, which is a cycleway, signed 'Chippenham 5'. Follow this round a left-hand bend and a right-hand bend.

⑥ When it bends right again by a disused canal, turn sharp left over a stile on a signed path. Follow the path by the old canal, then continue along the left-hand side of a field. At the end of the field the path crosses the field boundary to continue in the same direction along the right-hand side of a second field. At the end of this field, turn left round the perimeter to about 30 yards before the end.

The Wilts and Berks canal was proposed in 1793 and opened in 1810 to connect the Kennet and Avon canal with the Thames, near Abingdon. Ironically, its most profitable years were the 1830s because the canal provided an efficient means of transporting the vast quantities of iron, brick, stone, aggregate and timber needed to build the Great Western Railway, which, apart from the eastern and western extremities, is never more than a mile or two away from the canal. Thus the canal contributed towards its own eventual, and probably inevitable, decline and abandonment early in the 20th century.

7 Turn right through a metal barrier on a signed fenced path to a lane. Cross the lane and bear half left across a field to a stile onto another lane.

8 Over the stile turn right across a bridge over the river Avon, then turn left. When the lane shortly bends right, keep ahead on a surfaced track that leads to a surfaced path across a field.

9 At the far side of the field, turn left along a lane that leads across a ford to the teashop next to the church.

10 You may well wish to wander around the unspoilt medieval village of Lacock. The direct route back to the starting point is to turn left out of the teashop, then take the first street on the left. Turn left again at a T-junction. At the entrance to the abbey and the Fox-Talbot Museum, bear right on a path back to the car park.

One member of the Talbot family made a distinguished contribution to our contemporary world. William Henry Fox Talbot was a gentleman scholar who was one of the founders of modern photography. He invented the positive/negative process that allows multiple copies to be made. A museum about his life and work is located in a medieval barn at the entrance to Lacock Abbey. The abbey is open every afternoon except Tuesday between April and October. The museum is open every day between 11 am and 5 pm between March and October and most weekends in winter. Telephone: 01249 730459.

Walk 15

AVEBURY AND THE RIDGEWAY

*T*he pretty village of Avebury shares its setting among the Downs with one of the most significant megalithic monuments in Europe. The surrounding countryside has such a concentration of fine prehistoric monuments that it has been made a World Heritage Site and this fascinating walk approaches them as our ancestors would have done – on foot. Unlike at neighbouring Stonehenge, visitors can wander freely among the mysterious stones and even go right inside one of the structures. After refreshment at the excellent National Trust tearoom at Avebury, the route climbs steadily to one of the great ancient trade routes of Southern England. The final mile is a joy – a gentle descent with panoramic views all around. It is best to regard this as an all-day expedition as there is so much to see and speculate upon. The monuments have information boards so I have not replicated what they say.

The Avebury estate was donated to the National Trust in the 1940s and has created facilities for visitors in what was, until the 1970s, the farmyard of Avebury Manor. These include an interesting museum and display and the Circle Restaurant in old farm buildings. This has a light and modern interior and several tables outside overlooking what is now a pleasant grassed area with a pond. It serves a selection of baguettes and sandwiches, together with hot specials and an excellent choice of cakes including, on my visit, a rich and delicious tiffin. It is open throughout the year between 10 am and 5.30 pm from April to October and to 3.30 pm in the winter months. Telephone: 01672 539250.

DISTANCE: 6 miles, plus ½ mile optional extension to West Kennett Long Barrow

MAP: OS Explorer 157 Marlborough & Savernake Forest

STARTING POINT: Sanctuary and Ridgeway car park on the A4. Park on the north side of the A4. (GR 118681)

HOW TO GET THERE: The car park is signed on the A4, Marlborough–Calne road, about 3½ miles west of Marlborough.

ALTERNATIVE STARTING POINT: If you wish to visit the teashop at the beginning or end of your walk, start in Avebury where there is ample parking in the National Trust car park (charge) on the outskirts of the village. The teashop is in the village. You will then start the walk at point 6.

THE WALK

1 Return to the road and continue along a track opposite, signed 'Byway'.

2 As the track bends left, turn right on a clear path to walk along the left-hand side of a field to a lane.

3 Turn left for 70 yards, crossing the river Kennet, then turn right along an unsigned track. Watch for a path on the left opposite a stile on the right. Do not cross the stile but continue along the track for a further 20 yards to a waymarked path on the right.

4 Turn right along a fenced path to a stile. Over the stile, carry on along the left-hand side of a field, following the field boundary round to the left, to a stile next to a field gate onto a lane. Cross the lane and press on ahead on a signed path along a track. This soon leads into a field; continue along the right-hand side of the field to a path junction.

To visit West Kennett Long Barrow, turn left here for about ¼ mile gently uphill, then return to the same spot. (To continue with the route, keep ahead then follow the path as it turns right to the A4).

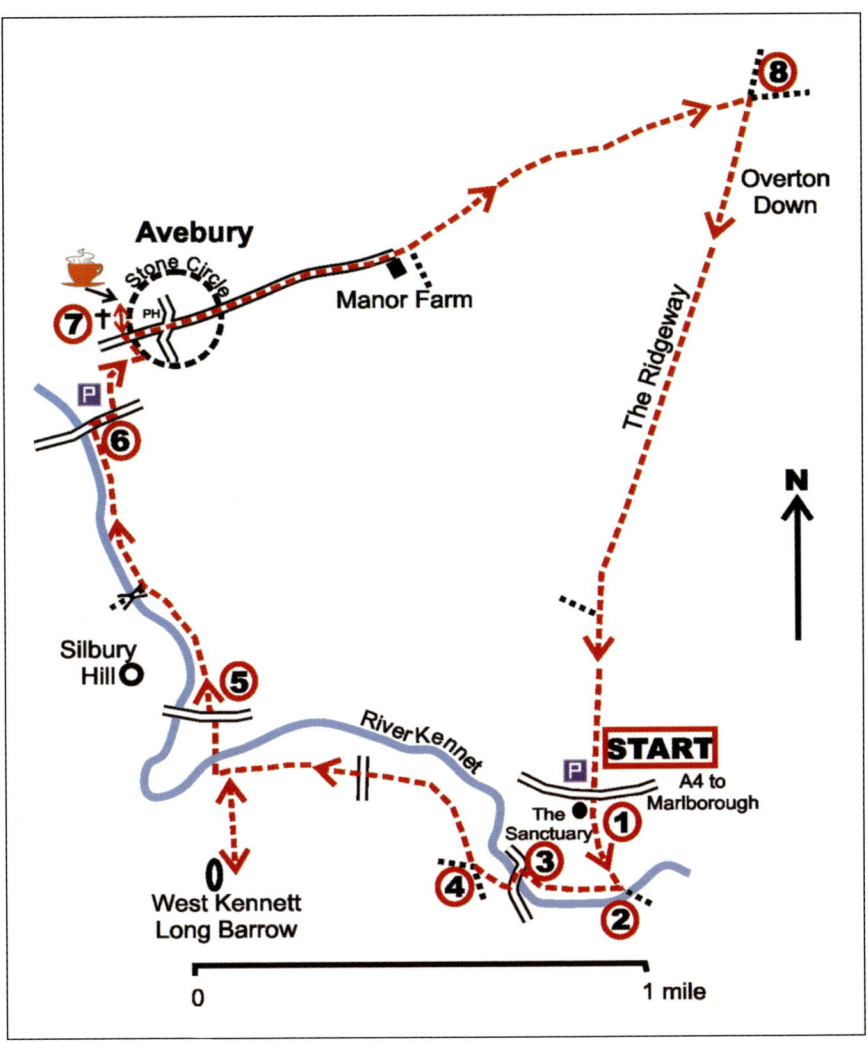

5 Cross the road and take a path 35 yards to the left, signed 'Avebury 1 mile', soon walking beside the river Kennet, with a fine view of Silbury Hill. Do not cross the bridge over the river but continue beside it to a road.

Silbury Hill is one of the most astonishing historical landmarks in England. At 130 ft high and covering an area of over five acres, the enormous contours of the hill still challenge us with the mystery of why it was built. All sorts of theories have been proposed, from a landing platform for an alien spaceship to a co-ordinating centre for ceremonies in the area, as the top is visible from a remarkable number of spots around. One thing is known: none of the numerous excavations have found the slightest trace of a burial.

Whatever it was – and we will probably never know for sure – it must have been important to the people of that time as it has been calculated that it took over four million man hours of labour to build, probably in three stages. It has been repeatedly excavated since the 18th century to try and uncover the secrets of this mysterious mound. This left voids within and in the year 2000, having survived over 4,000 years, a large hole over 50 ft deep appeared in the top and this led to a major project to stabilise the monument in 2007. There is much more information about Silbury Hill, and the other monuments, in the museum in Avebury, which is open throughout the year and is adjacent to the teashop. Telephone: 01672 539250.

6 Turn right for a few yards, then left through a car park to the far right corner. From here follow a surfaced path to the village. Cross a lane and follow a track to the teashop.

The evidence suggests that a permanent community here dates back no further than Saxon times. When the monuments were in active use, the village we now

Avebury's impressive stone circle.

know lay over 3,000 years in the future – a mind-boggling thought. Much of Avebury lies within the henge, and many stones have been smashed as an easy source of building material, to clear land for agriculture or because of religious sensibilities. Gradually, perceptions have changed from Avebury being a village near a mysterious and ancient stone structure to a site of world significance, with a village conveniently located to service the admiring visitors.

The village itself holds much of interest, including the church of St James, which has a long history going back 1,000 years. There is also a fine manor house, now in the care of the National Trust. It is occupied by private leaseholders, but part of it is open some summer afternoons. Telephone: 01672 539250.

7 From the teashop, return to the lane and turn left. Continue ahead at a road junction, passing Avebury Chapel Centre. The lane ends at Manor Farm. Carry on along the track, ignoring a track to the right just after the farm, to eventually meet a cross path at the top of the hill.

8 Turn right along the Ridgeway, signed 'Overton Hill', and follow this back to the car park.

The Ridgeway was one of the great prehistoric trade routes and ran between the Dorset coast and the North Sea, riding the back of the great chalk ridge across southern England. Its route is close to many sites that were significant during the Neolithic and Bronze ages and a number of prominent Iron Age sites are also to be found nearby. Its true age remains unknown and begs the question, 'Is Avebury where it is because of the Ridgeway or is the Ridgeway where it is because of Avebury?'

Another feature that allowed the building of so many stone monuments was the availability of suitable material and this can be seen from the path. In the fields to the left is a huge number of sarcen stones, also known locally as Grey Wethers, as from a distance they can resemble flocks of sheep (a wether is a castrated ram).

Walk 16

GREAT BEDWYN AND CROFTON

This excellent walk is attractive, varied and has something for everyone. In its few short miles it explores beautiful woods, treads waterside paths, passes through a pretty village with an abundance of thatched cottages, many complete with roses round the door, and offers the opportunity to study a wealth of fascinating industrial archaeology in a charming rural setting, rounded off by tea three-quarters of the way round. What could be better?

Crofton Pumping Station is open to the public throughout the summer but there is no doubt that a visit is even better when the magnificent old engines are in steam and you can experience close up the smell and sounds of these wonderful relics of our past. This is essentially the last weekend of every month and the Early May Bank Holiday weekend but for more details telephone 01672 870300 or visit their website at www.croftonbeamengines.org.

 The Engineman's Rest at Crofton Pumping Station is housed in the engine house and also has lots of tables outside to enjoy the splendid views across the canal to the hills and woods beyond. It serves a very good choice of tempting cakes supplemented by sandwiches and soup and is open every day except Wednesday between 10.30 am and 5 pm from Easter to the end of September. Telephone: 01672 870300.

When the teashop is closed the pub in Wilton, the Swan, serves food and there are also pubs in Great Bedwyn.

DISTANCE: 5 miles

MAP: OS Explorer 157 Marlborough & Savernake Forest

STARTING POINT: St Mary the Virgin church, Great Bedwyn (GR 277642)

HOW TO GET THERE: Great Bedwyn is signed from the A4 between Marlborough and Hungerford and from the A338 between Burbage and Hungerford. The church is at the south-west edge of the village on the road to Crofton.

ALTERNATIVE STARTING POINT: If you wish to visit the teashop at the beginning or end of your walk, start at Crofton Pumping Station where there is a car park (charge). The teashop is at the Pumping Station. You will then start the walk at point 7.

THE WALK

1 Facing the church, take a footpath at the right-hand side of the churchyard signed 'Bedwyn Brail $^1/_2$'. Follow the path through the churchyard extension and across a small field and the railway to a canal.

2 Cross the bridge over the canal and go through a gate ahead. Turn right for 75 yards, then turn left up a bank on a not very obvious path to a stile to walk along the right-hand side of two fields to a wood. Follow the clear path through the wood, across a clearing and keep ahead as it becomes a track. Continue in the same direction, signed 'Windmill', at a cross path and keep ahead at the next junction.

3 At the next signed cross path, turn right, signed 'Windmill', for 40 yards to a fork. Bear left, again signed 'Windmill', to a T-junction after 150 yards. Turn left to a lane.

4 Turn right along the lane, passing Wilton Windmill, to a T-junction.

The site is always open and information boards explain how it all worked. The mill itself is open between 2 pm and 5 pm on Sundays and Bank Holiday Mondays from Easter to the end of September. Telephone: 01672 870266.

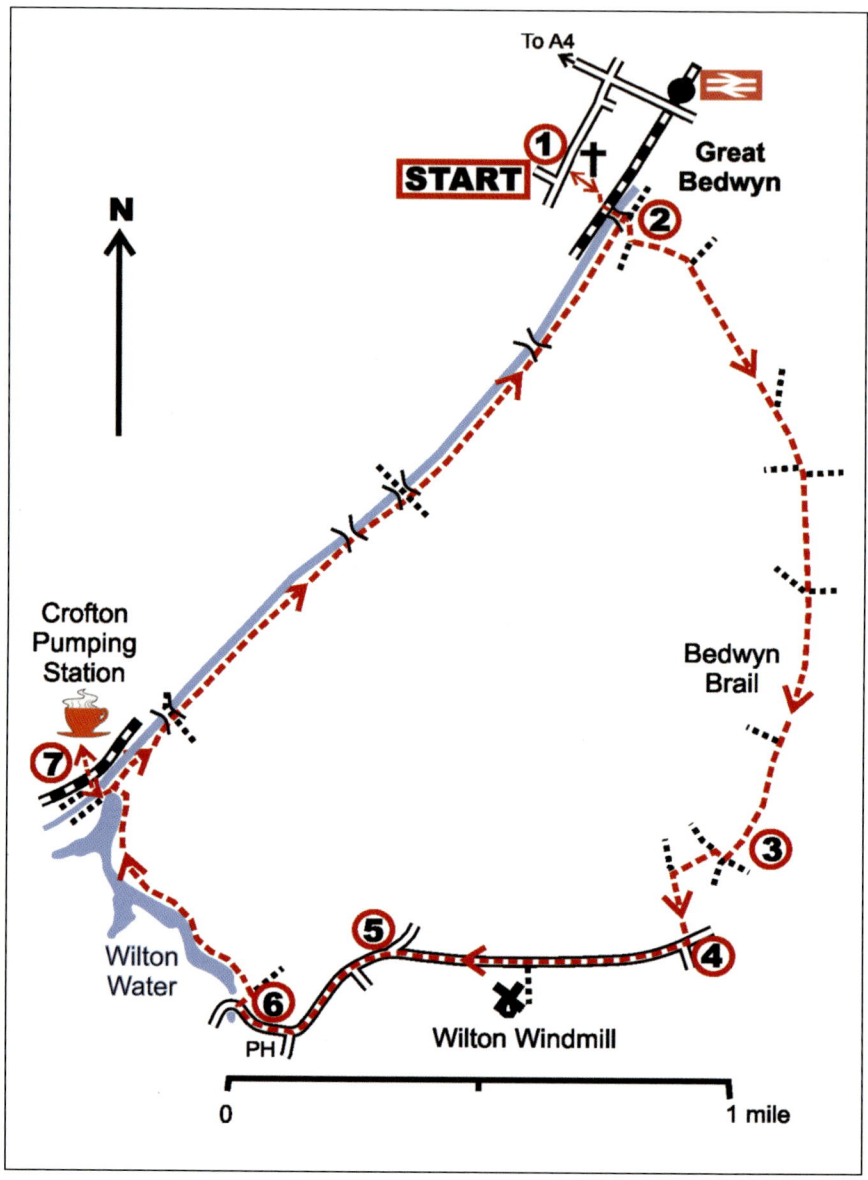

5 Turn left and walk down into Wilton. Follow the main road round to the right, signed 'East Grafton'.

6 Level with the village pond, turn right on a signed path along a track for 50 yards, then turn left on a signed path that leads to and then beside a small reservoir to the canal. Turn left for a few yards to cross the canal at the first lock, then walk under the railway and up some steps to the engine house and teashop.

When the Kennet and Avon canal was built in the early years of the 19th century there was no obvious and reliable source of water to replenish the losses at the summit. For that reason, as well as others, it is doubtful whether the canal should have come this way (see Walk 12). The problem was solved at considerable expense by taking water from two springs to a well sunk from the pumping station, which is built on the hillside more than 40 ft above the canal. The pumps take the water from the well and discharge it into a feeder channel next to the pumping station. The water flows along this channel by gravity until it reaches the summit pound about a mile to the west. The pumping station still houses two magnificent beam engines. One of these, the 1812 Boulton and Watt machine, is the oldest working beam engine in the world still in its original engine house and still capable of doing the work for which it was installed. The job is now carried out on a regular basis by electrically-powered pumps but these are switched off when the boilers are fired up and the beam engines take over. The reservoir, known as Wilton Water, was created some years later to make the water supply more reliable.

7 Retrace your steps to and across the canal and turn left along the towpath for 1 1/2 miles to the fifth bridge where you crossed the canal early in the walk. Leave the canal and retrace your steps back to the church and the start.

(If you started at Crofton Pumping Station, turn right at the bridge to pick up the directions at point 2.)

Walk 17

SAVERNAKE FOREST AND MARLBOROUGH

This route starts with a couple of miles through Savernake Forest and must be among the best woodland walking in the county, possibly in the south and arguably in England, as it passes many magnificent ancient oak and beech trees. On leaving the forest the route descends into the Kennet valley and the village of Mildenhall for a charming walk along the valley floor to Marlborough. This ancient, gracious and interesting town is worth taking the time to explore and has one of England's best-known tearooms, which has been refreshing visitors since the 1930s. The last, short leg involves a stiff climb out of the town but, fully restored by tea, it is not too arduous, especially if you pause to admire the ever-widening view behind.

The Polly Tearooms in Marlborough is a charming traditional establishment founded in 1932 by Miss Janet McCloud (one of the original Suffragettes) and Miss Jean Leith Hay. They named their teashop after Polly Peacham from *The Beggars Opera* and it has been delighting residents and visitors for over 70 years. The cream teas are excellent, with a choice of jams, or you can choose from a wide selection of cakes and pastries. Possibilities for lunch range from sandwiches, salads and filled jacket potatoes through light meals to full meals, served until 3.30 pm, such as roast salmon with crushed new potatoes and pea and dill sauce. Polly is open until 5 pm during the week and 6 pm at the weekend throughout the year. Telephone: 01672 512146.

There is no other source of refreshment other than in Marlborough , although the Horseshoe Inn at Mildenhall is not far off the route.

DISTANCE: 7 miles

MAP: OS Explorer 157 Marlborough & Savernake Forest

STARTING POINT: Postern Hill car park, Savernake Forest. This is an ill-defined area so the instructions start from the public conveniences. Note also that the car park is locked in the evening and you will be charged a hefty callout fee if you misjudge it and need someone to come and release you. (GR 198681)

HOW TO GET THERE: Postern Hill car park is signed from the A346, Marlborough to Salisbury road, about a mile south of Marlborough.

ALTERNATIVE STARTING POINT: If you wish to visit the teashop at the beginning or end of your walk, start in Marlborough where there are signed car parks. You will then start the walk at point 13.

THE WALK

Savernake Forest is rightly famous for its splendid avenues of tall 200-year-old beech trees, and these are seen at their best in October when the green leaves turn to glorious shades of gold, copper and brown. Several venerable trees are individually named, such as the Saddle Oak that the route passes. The forest was given to one of the victorious knights who fought at the Battle of Hastings in 1066, and since then it has passed down through 31 generations, never once being bought or sold in a thousand years. The family that own it from that day to this was called Seymour in Tudor times and was extremely influential. In the 19th century the head of the family inherited the title of Earl of Cardigan from a cousin and it is still owned by the Earl. Today it is the only such forest in Britain still in private hands though the timber rights are leased to the Forestry Commission.

1 With your back to the public conveniences, turn left along a track. Follow the main track round to the right and stay on it, ignoring all side tracks and paths and across a major cross path to eventually arrive at a T-junction with a surfaced drive.

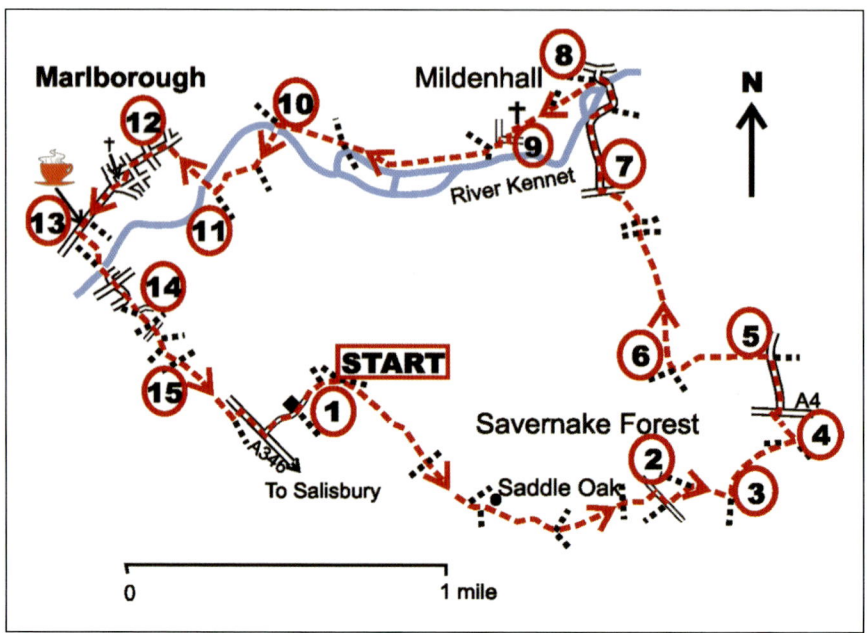

In the late 18th century, Lord Thomas Bruce became Governor to the young King George IV. He employed Capability Brown to plant great beech avenues through the forest, which was then some 40,000 acres, nearly ten times its present size. These included this surfaced drive, the Grand Avenue, running through the heart of the forest and which, at 4 miles long, appears in the Guinness Book of Records as the longest avenue in Britain.

2 Turn right for 100 yards, then turn left on a wide path. Walk along this, with a wire fence on the left, to a T-junction.

3 Turn left, still with the wire fence on the left, to eventually merge with a path coming in from the left near a gate, then keep ahead for 50 yards to a major track.

4 Turn left to the A4. Turn right for 30 yards then left along a lane, signed 'Stitchcombe', for a bare 1/4 mile to a cross track.

5 Turn left for 1/4 mile to a signed cross path.

6 Turn right and follow a hedged path. Press ahead across a track to join a lane.

7 Turn left for 25 yards, then right at the first junction down into Mildenhall to a bridge across the river Kennet.

Mildenhall stands close to the site of a significant Roman fort and town called Cunetio, a Latinised form of the name Kennet. It was at the junction of the roads from Cirencester to Winchester and from London to Bath: this path and lane, called Cock-a-troop Lane, is the road to Winchester. The curious name is nothing to do with Roman legions but is a corruption of Crokeres-trope, 'the potters' settlement', which testifies to the pottery industry in the area during the Saxon period. Nothing of the extensive Roman settlement now remains above ground but excavations have shown that it was occupied throughout the Roman period. Two associated hoards of Roman coins were discovered in 1978. A total of almost 55,000 coins had been hidden during the AD 270s, the largest hoard ever to have been discovered from Roman Britain, which suggests that Cunetio was a place that attracted the wealthy.

8 Some 50 yards after the bridge, turn left on a signed path that almost immediately leads onto a playing field. Walk along the left-hand side of this and the next two fields to find a gate into a churchyard. Go through the gate and press on to the left of the church to a drive from a farm.

Mildenhall is pronounced and often written as 'Minal' locally. The church was restored in 1816 by a group of local benefactors so its style is Georgian rather than the more familiar Victorian. It was a favourite of Sir John Betjeman who described it perfectly: 'You walk into the church of a Jane Austen novel, into a forest of magnificent oak joinery, an ocean of box pews stretching shoulder high all over the church.' Note the fine sundial on the tower.

The sundial on the church at Mildenhall.

9 Turn right and immediately turn left, then immediately right again to shortly reach a metal kissing gate. Do not take the signed path half right but take an unsigned path round the left perimeter of the field. Keep ahead along this clear path to some steps leading up onto a disused railway, now a cycleway. Go up the steps and down the other side, then follow the path to a plank bridge on the left.

⑩ Go across the bridge and follow the path ahead, taking the right option at a fork to a T-junction with a surfaced path.

⑪ Turn right to a road.

⑫ Turn left into Marlborough. At a main road bear half left on a path across The Green, then between houses and past a church and ahead along Patten Alley onto the High Street. Turn right along the High Street to the Polly Tearooms on the left.

Marlborough became the pre-eminent town of this part of Wiltshire when the Normans decided to build a castle here and transferred the mint from Great Bedwyn. The castle was an important residence for the king, and King John and later Henry III were married there. Henry III held Parliament at Marlborough in 1267, when the Statute of Marlborough was passed. This 700-year-old law states that no one shall seize his neighbour's goods for an alleged wrong, without permission of the Court. It is the oldest piece of English legislation still in force. It is worth taking the time to explore and a guide to the many interesting buildings can be obtained from the tourist information office on the High Street.

⑬ Turn left out of the teashop and immediately left under arches into Priory Gardens. Follow the path round the gardens to emerge on an alley. Turn left over the river. Keep ahead to a main road. Cross this and continue in the same direction up Ducks Meadow.

⑭ When the road bends right, keep ahead on a surfaced path. At the top of the hill cross the end of a road and continue ahead, soon crossing a track. Go across another road and again keep ahead. When the surfaced path shortly bends left, keep ahead on an unsurfaced path that leads down into a valley and up to a track.

⑮ Cross the track to a stile then maintain the same direction along the left-hand side of two fields, then ahead to a stile on the left.

⑯ Go over the stile and along a track to a road. Turn right for 200 yards to the entrance to the car park and campsite. Fork right after 25 yards, back to the start.

Walk 18

MALMESBURY

*M*almesbury is the oldest borough in England, having been granted its charter in AD 880 by King Alfred. It can lay claim to be the original capital of England and is built on the site of an Iron Age hill fort on a rocky promontory enclosed by two branches of the river Avon. This route starts below the hill on which the town is perched and explores the countryside downstream of the confluence, with pleasant stretches beside the river itself. It then climbs away from the river to the site of a relic of England's first, forgotten 12th-century civil war and a great view before approaching Malmesbury from the other side. Such a town exudes history from every brick and there is something of interest round every corner. There isn't space here to describe it all but if you are interested I suggest you visit the tourist information office by the short stay car park to pick up the walking guide to the town before you set off. A walk through the town and tea, combined perhaps with a visit to the abbey and the famous gardens adjacent, complete an interesting expedition. The route presents no problems but some short sections can be heavily fringed by exuberant nettles in summer, so something more substantial than shorts is advisable.

Amanda's in Oxford Street in the centre of Malmesbury offers a very good choice of cakes and other teatime treats, ranging from toasted teacakes to Sybil's Sublime Tea for two featuring smoked salmon sandwiches, scones with jam and clotted cream and cakes. Don't worry if you are tempted by this; it isn't far back to the start! Savoury food includes an all-day breakfast, an enormous range of sandwiches, salads and daily specials. Tea is served in unusual combination pots and cups. There is a very attractive walled garden at the back. It is open 9 am until 5 pm Monday to Thursday and closes at 4 pm at the weekend. Telephone: 01666 829356.

DISTANCE: 4½ miles

MAP: OS Explorer 168 Stroud, Tetbury & Malmesbury

STARTING POINT: Malmesbury long-stay car park (charge) (GR 932875)

HOW TO GET THERE: The car park is amply signed from the A429, Malmesbury–Cirencester road, and from the B4014, Malmesbury–Tetbury road.

ALTERNATIVE STARTING POINT: There is no long-stay car park closer to the teashop than the one suggested.

THE WALK

From this car park, once the site of Malmesbury's railway station, it is obvious what a great defensive position this promontory offers, surrounded on three sides by rivers, and why an Iron Age hill fort, a Saxon town and a Norman castle were all built here. Archaeological evidence suggests it had already been occupied for 2,000 years by the time the hill fort was built over two millennia ago.

1 Go to the far end of the car park and turn left. Almost immediately turn right through a kissing gate to the right of a private nature reserve car park, to walk through Conygre Mead Nature Reserve on a riverside path that leads to a road at a bridge.

2 Cross the road to a footpath between two branches of the river. When the branch on the left turns left, keep by the branch on the right to a stile by a gate. Over the stile, fork left over to the other branch to shortly cross it at a bridge to a lane.

3 Turn left. At a metal barrier keep ahead under a main road on a surfaced drive. When this ends, go over a stile to the right to continue in the same direction to a gate. Through the gate, press on along the right-hand side of

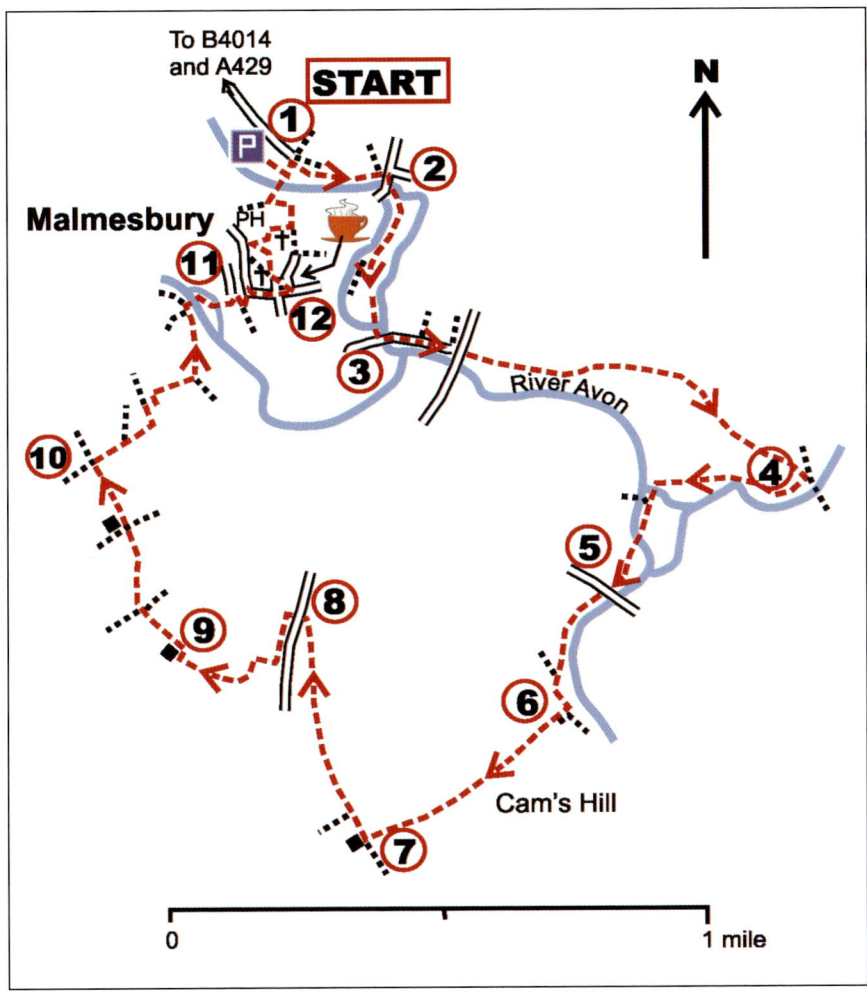

the field to a stile at the end into a second field. Maintain the same line across this second field to a stile on to a drive.

4 Do not cross the stile but turn right, almost back on yourself, to a river. Walk beside it for a short distance then, as you approach the end of the field, bear away to find a stile about 30 yards to the right of a gate. Over the stile, go ahead to find a bridge over a branch of the river at a weir, that leads to a stile by a gate onto a surfaced drive. Go ahead along the drive with the river on the right to eventually arrive at a main road.

5 Cross the road and take a signed path opposite, again by the river. When the river bends left, bear slightly away from the river up to a stile in the corner of the field, followed immediately by a second. Over the second stile turn left to another double stile.

6 Over these, turn right and walk uphill along the right-hand side of two fields, joining a track. At the top continue along the track down the other side to reach a cross track just before a farm.

The intriguing lumps and bumps at the top of the hill are the remains of a siege castle built in 1144, during the Civil War between Empress Matilda and her cousin Stephen for the throne of England.

7 Turn right. When the track bends left, keep ahead over three stiles and a plank bridge into a field. Continue across the field, heading for a gate. In the next field bear left to a stile onto a main road in the far left corner.

8 Turn left, using the footway on the right-hand side, for 170 yards. Turn right on a signed path, possibly supporting a vigorous crop of nettles, which leads to a stile into a field. Turn left for 180 yards. Just as a fence starts, look for a possibly overgrown stile on the left and cross this into a small field. Go diagonally across the field to a stile in front of a converted barn.

9 Pass to the right of the barn along a track that soon becomes a surfaced drive. When the drive bends right at a farm, leave the drive to continue in the same direction, passing to the right of the farm to shortly pick up a track.

10 Some 100 yards after the end of the farm buildings, go over a stile on the right by a metal field gate and head over to another stile in the far right corner. Now press on along the right-hand side of a field. At the end of this field, turn left for 30 yards to a stile on the right. Cross this stile and walk along the left-hand side of a field. At the end of the field turn left through a small wooden gate and walk along the right-hand side of a field to cross a stone bridge over one branch of the river. Now follow a stone path to another bridge and on to a T-junction.

There is an excellent view of the abbey from this path. It has had a long and chequered history and, especially as the route goes past it, is worth visiting.

The abbey has produced several notable sons. Aldhelm, a scholar and poet, founded it as a Benedictine house around AD 676. It is said that when the townspeople showed a lack of interest in the church, Aldhelm stood at the end of the bridge singing songs in the vernacular, to drum up a crowd to listen to his sermons. Another was the medieval historian, William of Malmesbury. From him we learn of Abbot Daniel, of whom he wrote: 'That he might reduce the force of his rebellious body, he used to immerse himself up to his shoulders in a spring near the monastery. There, caring neither for the frosty rigour of winter nor for the mists rising from the marshy ground in summer, he used to pass the night unharmed.' This path passes the site of Daniel's struggles with his unruly flesh. William also tells us about an early attempt at human flight when, in 1010, the monk Eilmer flew a primitive hang-glider from one of the abbey's towers. He flew over 200 yards before landing when he broke both legs and was crippled for life. Despite this he was convinced that the only reason he did not fly further was the lack of a tail on his glider and was prepared to have another attempt until forbidden by the abbot. William says that Eilmer mistook the Greek legend of Icarus for truth but it is also possible that he was inspired by stories of successful glider flights by Moorish inventors.

⑪ Turn right on a rising path, with a wall on the left and railing on the right, for 50 yards then turn left up steps. At the top go ahead along a road, passing the Market Cross, to the teashop on the left.

⑫ Turn right out of the teashop to return to the Market Cross and go through a gate into the abbey grounds. Walk across to a gate in front of the Old Bell. Turn right into Cloister Gardens and cross to the far left corner. Go down some steps. At the bottom, bear right across the river yet again to the car park where this walk started.

The entrance to Abbey House Gardens is from the Cloister Gardens. The gardens have been created by Ian and Barbara Pollard who are known as 'The Naked Gardeners' from the way they like not to dress. One wonders about thorns and biting insects? The gardens are open daily from 21 March to 31 October between 11 am and 5.30 pm. The Pollards dress for visitors except on pre-arranged 'clothes optional days'. Telephone: 01666 822212.

Walk 19

COTSWOLD WATER PARK

This level walk straddles the border of Wiltshire and Gloucestershire, crossing and recrossing it. The Thames has deposited gravel beds along its valley and these have been dug out for use as a building material. In the 1960s the local authorities realised what a great resource this industry had bequeathed them and created the 12,000 hectare Cotswold Water Park, comprising some 140 lakes. This route explores part of this watery landscape, using the line of an old railway and a canal towpath so the going is easy and makes a very pleasant walk. There is also a short stretch by the infant river Thames. If you enjoy waterside walking, this is certainly one for you and it is a superb example of how a once industrial landscape can be transformed. A gravel extraction pit is not a pretty sight when the diggers are at work, but as extraction ceased they were flooded with clean spring water and have become a haven for wildlife and fishermen.

🍵 Coots, in the visitor centre for Cotswold Water Park, is a wonderfully airy place that combines traditional aspects such as cruck beams with modern features including solar panels on the roof. The windows overlook one of the lakes and there are also a few tables outside – a delightful place to sit and enjoy a slice of cake while watching the antics of the coots and other birds. Cream teas and delicious cakes are served; on my visit I enjoyed a particularly moreish rhubarb cake. For lunch there is a wide range of sandwiches and baguettes, together with salads and filled jacket potatoes. Don't forget to have a look at the amazing fossil discovered locally. Coots is open every day between 9 am and 5 pm. Telephone: 01285 862962.

DISTANCE: 6 miles

MAP: OS Explorer 169 Cirencester & Swindon

STARTING POINT: Bridge car park (GR 063962)

HOW TO GET THERE: From the A419 Swindon–Cirencester road, about 3 miles north of Cricklade, take the B4696 towards Ashton Keynes for 1 mile to a signed car park on the right, reached through some brick arches.

ALTERNATIVE STARTING POINT: If you wish to visit the teashop at the beginning or end of your walk, start at the visitor centre on the B4696 near its junction with the A419 where there is a large car park. You will then start the walk at point 5.

THE WALK

① Return to the road and go ahead through a gate opposite on a wide, hedged path. Follow this for about 1¹/₂ miles to where the Thames Path joins from the right at a fingerpost signed 'Ashton Keynes 3 m' to the right and 'Cricklade 1¹/₂ m' straight on. Keep ahead at this point for about 350 yards and watch for a signed path to the left.

Swindon is renowned among railway enthusiasts as the headquarters of the GWR – the Great Western Railway (or God's Wonderful Railway!), but this is the trackbed of Swindon's other, and much less well-known railway, the Midland and South Western Junction. This railway was built in the 1880s to link the industrial Midlands with the south coast. It was strongly opposed by the GWR who did not welcome competitors on what they regarded as their fiefdom. It was taken over by the GWR in 1923, when many staff left rather than serve under the 'old enemy'. Despite playing a key role in the preparations for D-Day in 1944, the line continued to be run down and passenger services were withdrawn in 1961.

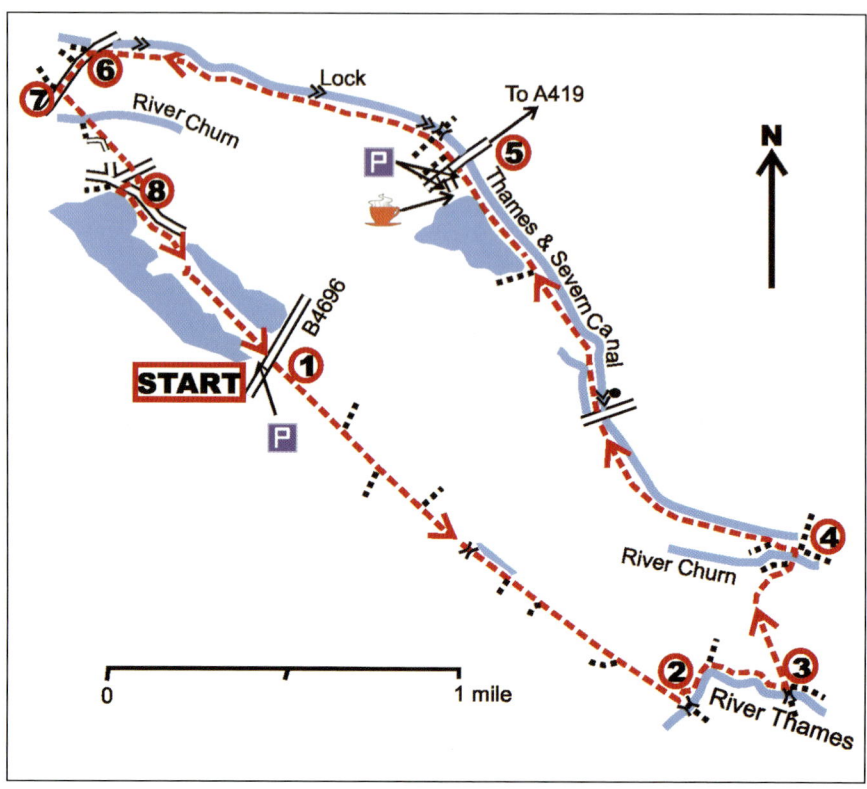

2 Turn left along a track signed 'Thames Path Cricklade 1½ m', to shortly walk beside the river. When the track turns left, keep on the path by the river along the right-hand side of a field.

3 At the end of the field turn left away from the river along a hedged path*. Continue ahead as the path joins a drive from a house.

* Ahead of you and accessible from this point is North Meadow National Nature Reserve, famous for its birds and wild flowers, including the rare snake's head fritillary. The traditional management of this type of hay meadow allows a very diverse range of plants to thrive but has been superseded in most places by modern intensive agriculture. The snake's head fritillary, for example, used to be widespread across southern England but now this one meadow may be home to as much as 80% of the British population. It has continued under traditional management because the Enclosure Act of 1814 affecting the

district, which paved the way for intensive agriculture, specified that the meadow was to remain the property of the people of Cricklade and defined its use.

The path follows the line of the abandoned North Wilts canal, completed in 1819 to link the Wilts and Berks canal at Swindon (see Walk 14) to the Thames and Severn canal at Latton. A stop lock was built at the junction, together with a large basin to facilitate movement between the canals. This is currently undergoing restoration (is there any abandoned canal that is not the focus of a labour of love by a restoration group?) and information boards explain how it all worked.

④ Immediately after crossing a river, turn left over a stile next to a metal field gate. (If you start to climb to a bridge over the main road you have missed the turn!) There is now the river Churn on the left and the disused Thames and Severn canal bed on the right. A few yards after an information board, bear right to walk beside the canal and keep on this for 1¹/₂ miles, crossing a lane. When buildings come into view on the left and immediately after crossing a concrete bridge, bear left away from the canal to the teashop in the visitor centre.

The Thames and Severn canal was built to connect the two great rivers of England. It was a challenging project with 44 locks in 29 miles and an ambitious 2-mile tunnel at the summit. Its history is a familiar story: initially prosperous, it fell prey to competition from the railways and became derelict, with the last recorded through trip in 1911. It is now undergoing restoration and in the fullness of time it is hoped to reopen the entire length. Note the round house passed on the right. These are unique to the Thames and Severn and were built at the same time as the canal for workmen who combined the duties of watchman, lengthsman looking after part of the canal, and lock-keeper. It is now a private residence.

⑤ Turn right out of the visitor centre to retrace your steps to the canal and turn left, to carry on along the towpath beneath two bridges and beside three disused locks to a lane.

⑥ Turn left along the lane for about 300 yards.

⑦ Immediately after walking across a bridge, go down some steps on the right. Cross a plank bridge at the bottom and go ahead a few yards, then turn right along the track under the lane. Eventually this reaches the arches

The Thames and Severn Canal.

of another bridge. Turn right in front of them, then left through the last arch and continue along the path to a road.

8 Cross the road and turn left along a fenced path to walk with a lake on the right and initially the road on the left. This leads back to the car park where this walk started.

Gravel extraction began in this area over 50 years ago and is still going on today. When extraction is complete, the pumps are switched off and the holes fill naturally with water. So far, 147 lakes have been made in this way, used as wildlife havens and for all manner of water sports. Between permission for extraction and the start of quarrying, archaeologists look for evidence of human activity and this has resulted in the water park becoming, archaeologically, the most researched part of Britain. Remains from over 6,000 years of human activity have been found, from the early Stone Age, through the Bronze and Iron Ages, the Roman and Medieval eras, to modern times. During extraction, palaeontologists search for fossils in and under the gravel and many from the Jurassic period and Ice Age have been found, including the impressive mammoth skull on display in the visitor centre.

Walk 20

HANNINGTON AND HIGHWORTH

*I*n the far north of Wiltshire the rolling downs that are so much a feature of the county give way to the valley of the fledgling Thames. This route explores the edge of the downs and there are some magnificent views to the north, especially on the return leg to Hannington. The walk also visits Highworth, an old town graced by many fine Georgian buildings, that gets its name from its commanding hilltop position. The paths are well signed and easy to follow, though the bridleways used at the start can be uncomfortably muddy in a wet winter. However, it is not difficult to escape the worst of it and the going soon improves.

Sally's on the High Street in Highworth meets the needs of the local community and is a particularly good place for lunch. It serves an excellent selection of filled baguettes: the sausages from the butcher across the road are particularly sustaining and tasty. These are complemented by delicious cakes. Unusually, tea is served in over-sized cups rather than by the pot. Downstairs is tiny but there are some more tables upstairs and a couple outside where you can watch the world go by. Sally's is open every day throughout the year, opening at 7 am and closing at 4 pm during the week and between 8 am and 3 pm on Saturday and Sunday. Telephone: 01793 861871.

DISTANCE: 5¹/₂ miles

MAP: OS Explorer 169 Cirencester & Swindon

STARTING POINT: The village of Hannington, where there are several spots where a car can be left without causing inconvenience. The directions are given from the junction of the main road through the village and Skinners Close. (GR 176932)

HOW TO GET THERE: From the A419, Swindon–Cirencester road, take the B4019 towards Highworth. At the Freke Arms take a minor road north, signed 'Hannington 1 Castle Eaton 4', to Hannington, watching for Skinners Close on the left.

ALTERNATIVE STARTING POINT: If you wish to visit the teashop at the beginning or end of your walk, start in Highworth where there is a signed car park near Market Square. The teashop is on the High Street leading from Market Square. You will then start the walk at point 10.

THE WALK

1 With your back to Skinners Close, turn right along the main road through Hannington for 25 yards. Turn right along Home Farm Lane for 60 yards, then bear right off the lane on a hedged bridleway and follow this to a T-junction.

2 Turn left. Ignore a bridleway on the right signed 'Blunsden' and continue to a T-junction.

3 Turn left and follow the track to a lane.

4 Turn right along the lane. At a T-junction at the Freke Arms, turn left along the B4019, signed 'Highworth 1, Lechlade 7', for 75 yards.

5 Turn right along a track. Bear right after 30 yards on a wide, hedged path, soon passing a newly-planted copse on the right. At the end of the copse, keep ahead on a path with a hedge on the left for two fields to a T-junction at the end of the second field.

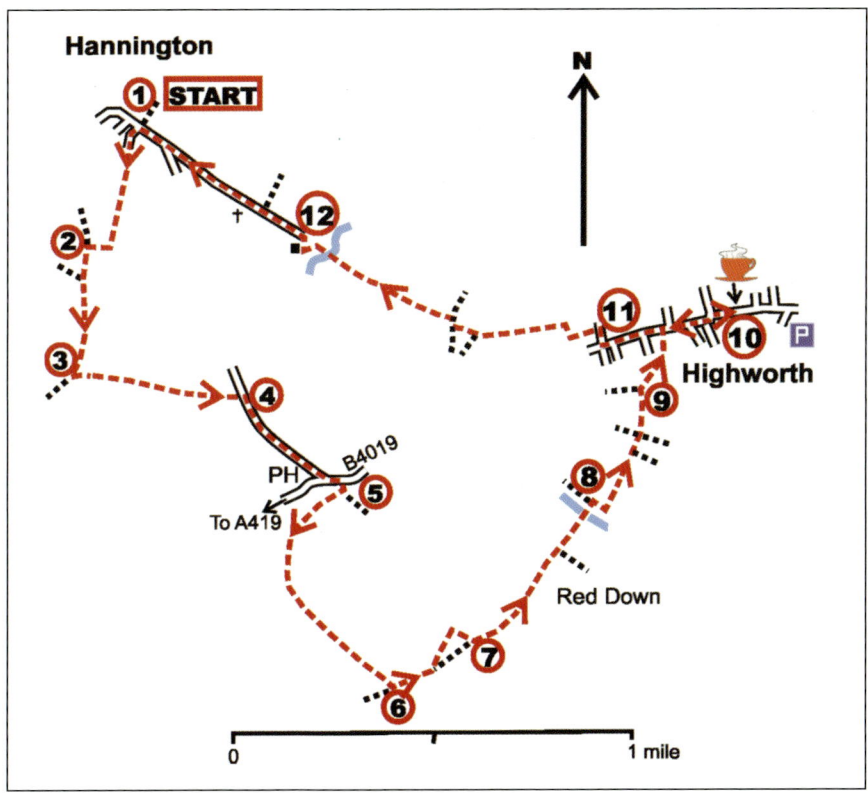

6 Turn left gently uphill and walk along the left-hand side of the field to its end, then turn right for 100 yards. (The right of way is shown across the field but in practice lies round the perimeter.)

7 Turn left and follow the way-marked path to a gate on to a golf course. Keep ahead, following the waymarks to a small bridge over a stream, then ahead a few yards to a gap in a hedge.

From this path there are panoramic views of the surrounding countryside and the commanding position of Highworth is clear. Archaeological and documentary evidence suggests that the hilltop on which Highworth sits has been almost continuously occupied for about 4,000 years. Bronze Age, Roman and Romano-British remains have been found on and around its hilltop. The Domesday Book refers to Wrde *or* Worth, *meaning a farmstead or enclosure and the epithet 'High' was added as the town grew in importance.*

8 Through the gap, turn right for 70 yards then turn left, again waymarked. Keep ahead to the end of the golf course, changing from the right of a hedge to the left as you approach some allotments.

9 At the end of the golf course, go through a gate on the right and bear half right across a recreation area to find a short paved path leading to a road. Turn right to some traffic lights, then continue more or less ahead along the High Street to the teashop on the left.

10 Turn right out of the teashop to walk back along the High Street to the main road. Cross the road and retrace your steps along Cricklade Road.

Continue past where the path joined the road for a further 270 yards to Bydemill Gardens.

Note: Westrop House and Cottage on the right on Cricklade Road. These have a system of tunnels which went from the large house to nearby stable buildings. They were used by servants who needed to keep themselves out of the limelight and incorporated a deep ice house where apparently ice could be kept for up to three years. Special niches were built into the walls to house bees during the winter and the passageways have air vents that lead up into the garden. Not surprisingly, the tunnels are said to have a resident ghost – the mistress of the man who built them.

11 Turn right for 30 yards then left on a signed path that soon leads beside and then across a cemetery. Leave through a gate and follow the path ahead across a field. In a second field do not follow the obvious path bearing left but fork right to a stile onto a track. Cross the track and press on along a path 10 yards to the right to eventually arrive at a stile into a farmyard.

12 Over the stile, go ahead to a farmhouse and turn right in front of it along a drive. This soon becomes a lane leading past Hannington church. The lane is lined with trees, some ancient and some more recent replacements. At a main road turn right into Hannington and back to the start.